About the author

Jacky Trevane, a Lincolnshire lass born and bred, has led a colourful life, to put it mildly. Her first book, *Fatwa* (2004), a bestseller, details the ten years spent in Egypt in the 80s as a twenty-something, living in the midst of a culture completely alien to her. Girlfriend evolved into wife, then mother.

Many years and experiences down the line, she now lives in Spain; older, hopefully wiser, still positive and a go-getter. *Tinderella* says it all.

TINDERELLA

Online Dating: Frogs, Fraudsters, Perverts or Princes?

JACKY TREVANE

TINDERELLA

Online Dating: Frogs, Fraudsters, Perverts or
Princes?

Vanguard Press

VANGUARD PAPERBACK

© Copyright 2022
Jacky Trevane

A CIP catalogue record for this title is
available from the British Library.

ISBN 978 1 80016 399 7

*Vanguard Press is an imprint of
Pegasus Elliot MacKenzie Publishers Ltd.*
www.pegasuspublishers.com

First Published in 2022

Vanguard Press
Sheraton House Castle Park
Cambridge England

Printed & Bound in Great Britain

Dedication

For Chloe

Something to make you smile

Something to remember your Nanny

Something to pay forward

Something to pass down the family

Big hug

Contents

Acknowledgements 11

PROLOGUE ONCE UPON A TIME 13

CHAPTER 1 Swipe Right 15

CHAPTER 2 You Are Who You Were 19

CHAPTER 3 Someone Should Write a Manual 23

CHAPTER 4 50 Shades 27

CHAPTER 5 It's a Date! 32

CHAPTER 6 Santa Claus and Secret Spies 38

CHAPTER 7 Would YOU Pay for It? 45

CHAPTER 8 Ripples in a Perfect Puddle 52

CHAPTER 9 The Big Bad Wolf: Covid-19 61

CHAPTER 10 Lockdown 73

CHAPTER 11 A Little of What You Fancy. 85

CHAPTER 12 Scheherazade 94

CHAPTER 13 Ogres and Trolls 107

CHAPTER 14 The Pied Piper with Red Flags 131

CHAPTER 16 Fairy Godmother, Wave your Magic

Wand! 150

CHAPTER 17 Pearls of Wisdom 155

CHAPTER 18 Rapunzel 166

CHAPTER 19 Timon and Pumbaa: Hakuna Matata

.... 176

CHAPTER 20 Hidden in Plain Sight 186

Acknowledgements

First and foremost, a huge thank you to my loyal, trusty team of readers; namely, Sandra, Maggie, Lizzie, Llana, Philomena, Tracey and Susan. You have stuck with me throughout, chapter by chapter, providing invaluable feedback across the board.

Without Daisy and Orla, the ending could have been very different. Thank you to you both.

To every single Frog, I salute you.

As for the Fraudsters, by coming under my radar, you enabled me to expose you as the scumbags you really are and in doing so, raise awareness significantly.

Friends through Tinder, you know who you are, how much I appreciate you and value our new-found friendship.

I can't leave out the Perverts. We all know you exist, and for me at least, you were the source of great amusement. You certainly added that *je ne sais quoi* to the story.

Finally, to my *PP, Anthony, I can say only this. If there is a storm ahead, let the sunlight pass through the raindrops and form a rainbow above us. Let our future be a rainbow full of colour and fun. That would be a welcome first.

Potential Prince

PROLOGUE
ONCE UPON A TIME

Present day: November 2020, global pandemic, second wave, Covid-19.

Have you ever heard the analogy from the Mental Health Foundation: "We are all in the same storm, but not all in the same boat"? It pins the coronavirus down quite well, I think. Simply put, it stretches all the way across the widescreen of society, disregarding and blind even to age, race, religion and income; across the full spectrum, in fact. Like a soggy blanket. Each of us was thrown into the ocean and had to deal with it, for better or worse, whether in a yacht, a dinghy or clinging to driftwood.

It must have been just three or four months before the emergence of Covid-19 and the first lockdown. I was sitting in the lounge with my two daughters. Capture the scene: Amira, thirty-five, staying temporarily with me after an extremely painful breakup with her boyfriend, withdrawn and shellshocked; Leila, thirty-nine, single and fine with it; and me, sixty-something, separated for just over a year, starting over in a new home in Spain.

'Oh, for heaven's sake, cheer up!' Leila was only visiting for a week and the oppressive mood in the air was difficult to ignore. 'There's plenty more fish in the sea.'

Amira inhaled and replied with yet another of her usual long, hopeless sighs.

'Stop going on about it. It just makes things worse. Anyway, I'm going on Tinder. Let's see who's out there.'

Leila's face lit up.

'Great idea. I know what — let's all go on it. Come on, Mum. It'll be a laugh. Let's see how many matches we can get in an hour.'

First of all, I didn't know what she was on about. And when the penny dropped, I was horrified. Second of all, I had a full, exciting, single life to get on with, so that was the last thing on my list for a bright, happy future.

I'm a strong-minded, independent woman. I can hold my own in discussions. There was no way on this earth I was going to get involved.

Thirty minutes later, we were all registered on Tinder, good to go. Hey ho. Just another female, sixty-something with convictions of steel. Not!

That was a year ago now. Looking back, I realise the exact same analogy can be applied to online dating: for those who choose to dip their toe in the water, we are all in the same storm, but not all in the same boat.

CHAPTER 1
Swipe Right

So there we were, unwittingly laying the foundations for the creation of a whole brave new world.

Never before having either thought or talked about dating sites, I started off as an extremely naive member of Tinder, a virgin online dater, ready to work hard, even kiss a few frogs, explore many tributaries and waterfalls, even ride the rapids before finding the river leading to my Prince Charming. Like Cinderella, my experience was far from smooth; in fact, really rocky at times. Why naive? Because I'm from the 'innocent-until-proven-guilty' brigade; 'trust until you show me you can't be trusted.' I would have been better advised to come at the whole thing from the opposite perspective. You know the one: 'Never trust anyone.'

Both girls stressed that I had to choose a username and never use my real name. That's a bit off, I thought: dishonest from the off? But no, they had to gently pull me into the present age of technology, identity theft, fraud and debauchery, until I changed my chip. I realised I had to take their advice on board. Rushing madly in, all open and honest, was more dangerous than a kamikaze mission. Plain as day now: clear as mud then.

'It's not for the good guys out there, Mum,' Amira stressed. 'It's for all the scumbags. And believe me, the scumbags come in all different forms and far outnumber the definite maybes. Think of it as your insurance, self-protection.'

Together we ploughed through the filters, stipulating age range, location of our 'perfect match.'

Can I put in 'no pink shirts?' (I really don't like pink shirts.)

'Really, Mum? Really?'

We were having fun for the first time in ages. The general mood was so much lighter and soon enough, my account was all set up and good to go.

For something that began as a bit of a laugh, it evolved into a whole alternate world, like a parallel universe. Funny how, within an hour, Amira had more than three hundred matches — yes, that's right — three bloody hundred. Leila was up there too and I had— go on, guess. How many? Zero matches.

I was relieved, to be honest. It was all a bit nerve-wracking. We skimmed through the matches the girls were getting, laughing like mad at some of them, and I have to admit, it was fun.

Only when we stopped for dinner, did they turn their attention to me.

'Show us your matches, Mum. Come on.'

'How many have you got?'

'I don't have any yet. Remember I'm from the wrinkly generation. There probably aren't any older members.'

Amira picked up my mobile. 'Don't be daft. There are loads. Let's have a look. How many — give or take — did you right-swipe?'

'Right-swipe?'

***

Long story short, I had looked at the photos after adding my filters, and swiped them all to the left. Mega blonde moment, absorbed in the photos, the idea of it, the variety of guys, etc. I was blown away by the mere concept. These were out there somewhere: possible dreamboats, real human beings. Crikey! My little brain hadn't got around to thinking about whether I liked them or not.

'Erm… none of them.'

'Doh! Well if you don't "like" them, you can't get a match! Anyway, you were right, you don't need to be on a site like that. So maybe it's for the best.'

Amira got up and sat on the sofa again, scrolling through her matches.

Too late. Curiosity ignited. Seed sown. Damn it, I had to take it further. Just to see.

Later that night, in the safety of my bedroom, I logged on to Tinder for another go.

'Now then,' I muttered to myself. I needed to concentrate. Gotta get this right. How do I remember which is which? Let's say, left for "let's leave" and right for "Mr Right". Okay then, let's get this show on the road. Online dating, I have arrived!

CHAPTER 2
You Are Who You Were

Nature or nurture? A biggie.

Personally, I truly believe we are who we are today as a result of how deeply past, negative experiences have affected us, whether we let them fester at the forefront of our minds, making us bitter and unable to see the bigger picture; lock them away in a box in the darkest corner of our mind never to be opened; or confront them, deal with them and move on.

Of course, this is always balanced out by the positive aspects and it is precisely how we respond, how equipped we are to do this, that shapes our character into the people we are today.

If all that sounds pretty involved, well — it's only half the story. Throw that into the mix with the "nature" perspective, the person you are innately, the characteristics which define you no matter what, and we can understand the wisdom of the words, "Everyone is unique."

Therefore, for the fifty-somethings, never having grown up around mobiles, tablets or iPads, online dating is a far more daunting challenge than for younger generations; in fact, way out of our comfort zone. Off the radar. The youth of today have the upper hand; a massive head start. The screens they all fixate on these days are as comfy to their world as wellies were to us.

Yes, you heard right: good old wellington boots! It rains a lot in England. All year round. And one of our favourite things was to pull on our wellies, go and stomp about in the puddles, play Pooh Sticks in the stream, have snowball fights, slide down hills on a plank of wood as a makeshift sledge, trudge up the muddy lane to the corner shop, kicking wet autumn leaves around. We wouldn't have survived without wellies.

Today, screens are the new wellies.

All of that set me apart from my two daughters. Born and raised in the north of England, I had a privileged upbringing. Not in economic terms, yet emotionally super-rich, surrounded by doting parents and two sets of grandparents, who together made sure they formed the fabric of a soft, fluffy, warm, invincible safety blanket.

The nurture part.

My nature? Predominantly curious, friendly, respectful, an urge to please those around me, to do well. Stubborn. As an adult, I floundered between relationships, mostly long-term, until admitting defeat and leaving. By the grand old age of sixty, I had two daughters, Leila and Amira; a son, Adam; and a granddaughter, Chloe. Leila, Chloe and Adam live in England, and Amira is a Spanish resident, like me. Before separating from my husband and setting up home just north of Granada, I lived in Zaragoza for twelve years. It's a stunningly beautiful, unspoilt city, essentially Spanish, which spreads out along the mouth of the River Ebro. Granada is another breath-taking city, famous for its palace, the Alhambra, and of course flamenco, nestling in the foothills of the Sierra Nevada mountains. A fresh start, even at my age. I felt enthusiastic, optimistic, ready. No man would get his pipe and slippers over my doorstep. Ever again.

It was fine for the first, frenzied months of restoration, painting, furniture hunting, exploring the local area, making new friends, job hunting, entertaining all the friends who visited. I considered myself happy. Amira landing on my doorstep a year ago simply meant that one became two. Double delight, I thought. Win-win. Even when Leila flew over for a short visit, and the subject of online dating was put out there, I never took it seriously — not for a second. This was probably my last chance to create the independent, free life I had always dreamed of: full of laughter, new experiences, my family, friends and their love. This was the utopia I had my heart set on. I certainly had no illusions, or delusions even, of browsing online for my Prince Charming.

What I failed to realise was that this scenario was just like a Polo mint. It had a hole in the middle, a central flaw. Romantic love. I thought I could live without it. I was a thousand percent sure. I was wrong. Oh boy, did I have a lot to learn. This particular Cinderella was about to meet every one of the seven dwarves, several Pinocchios and a couple of big, bad wolves into the bargain. If only I had had an inkling of what was to come.

CHAPTER 3
Someone Should Write a Manual

At first, I "right-swiped" every third or fourth guy. I mean, with Tinder, you don't actually get to chat with a guy unless he right-swipes you, too, and you have what they call a "MATCH."

Big mistake. When the green phrase "IT'S A MATCH!" flashes across the photo, then you start chatting. Well, obviously. But what I hadn't thought about, was the huge infringement it could have on your normal routine. For me, it started that very evening, in my bed. I became engrossed in the game, chatting to God only knows. It got to the point where I started mixing them up. Some English, some Spanish. It invaded my night, my sleep. Plus, I wasn't even enjoying it: I had been sucked into that auto-pilot state, flicking from one to another, answering inane questions, at random, to this one, then that one, until they gradually fused into one. It was only when I went to the bathroom and glanced out of the window, I realised it was already light outside. Half-past seven, in fact.

What the—? Had I actually been Tindering all night? What was that about?

Sitting there, on the loo, shivering a little as my body reacted to having been dragged out from under the duvet, I contemplated the advantages of this new hobby.

Let's see... Banging headache, screen blindness, lack of sleep, fingers getting cramp from so much texting, and that's just for starters.

There were obvious knock-on effects, like the fact I would be going around like a zombie, one-word grunts, dragging my feet in a hazy daze the following day, so that was a whole day lost, as well.

So none of that was what you might even remotely describe as advantageous. More like disastrous. Just think if you did this malarkey every day... Oh my days! I needed a rethink.

Shivering, I quickly washed my hands, raced barefoot back into bed and pulled the pillow over my head. I'd give myself an hour to try and catch some shut-eye and then make a plan. Reaching out, I felt for my mobile.

Right, you're going on silent for a bit, while I get chance to take a breath.

***

What seemed like two nanoseconds later, the alarm burst into my perfect dream world, shattering my peace and projected me firmly into reality. Blimey, that went quickly, I thought. I had, in fact, slept for a full hour.

Zombie alert. I searched in vain for my other slipper. I need tea.

This was far more complicated than I had first thought. I mean, hobbies take up time, I knew that. But if you already do stuff during the day, then you have to make extra time for them, like a cookery class or going to the gym. But this was not fixed and could easily take over and invade my comfy life, which so far, although work in progress, was actually coming on very nicely, thank you very much.

I stared down into my mug of tea. 'You need a manual for all this,' I stated seriously. 'Twenty-four hours in, and here I am: not yet dressed, one slipper on, my phone on silent to give me a break from the incessant messages coming through. I could just jack it all in, but I know my interest has been piqued and that's not gonna happen.'

I gave a huge sigh. 'And to cap it all, I'm now talking out loud to a cup of bloody tea. Get a grip, girl!'

As far as I know, there is no such thing as a manual for online dating sites. You know: a step-by-step handbook, telling me how to organise my time, how to get beyond the pitfalls and enjoy the perks, how to recognise a Big Bad Wolf at thirty paces and find my Prince Charming, wandering around with a lost slipper. 'Yes, hello! Over here! That would be mine! I'm in it to win it and I'm so not going to let it get the better of me.'

Seemed like I had decided to go for it anyway, so I did what I usually do.

I had another cuppa and made a plan, in the form of a list.

1. When you're not enjoying it, stop.
2. A maximum of an hour a day.
3. Be careful with the personal info you give out.
4. Try and meet for a date sooner than later to avoid all the insane messaging.

Mmm, that should do it. I can always add more along the way. Right, let's see who's out there.

CHAPTER 4
50 Shades

I now think the funniest, most entertaining part is the initial browsing. I mean, that first day, I clicked on every attractive photo I encountered.

I clicked on the message page, where there were seventeen new matches. Quite exciting. And then…

Hang about. What's this? Twenty-four years old? And this one — thirty-two? There must be some mistake. Can't you see, it clearly states on my profile that I am the grand old age of sixty-four! What is WRONG with you people?

Okay, calm down. You can't right-swipe based on their photo alone. Look at their age, etc. That should narrow it down a bit.

I was relieved to see that on every guy's profile page, you can click the little blue icon in the top right-hand corner and choose to either report them or "unmatch" them.

The next hour, tea stony cold — again — I dutifully unmatched every damned one. But hey, I have a microwave to heat up my tea and to be honest, it sort of felt like a cleansing experience, so not all bad.

Fresh start. Off we go again. There must be filters you can apply. Leila and Amira had set it up with me, but something was amiss if these guys were slipping through the net. I clicked on "Settings" to check out the filters.

Yes! Men or women? That's a good one, lol. Preferred language? Okay. I'll put Spanish down. Maximum distance? Mmm, eighty kilometres. Aah, here we are: age range. So I choose fifty-six to sixty-six. Nah, of course Tinder won't let me. At the top end of the age line is simply "fifty-five plus." So what that's supposed to mean is anyone's guess. I had no other option; I clicked on fifty-five plus.

Okay then, let's browse.

Well, I must say the filters certainly helped. First of all, they were fifty-five plus. So that instantly became more interesting and less of a time-waster. The distance filter didn't seem to be working, but now I was aware of that, I'd make a mental note to read where they lived. Anyway, maybe it wasn't such a bad idea to have a relationship with someone a fair way away. At this point I was open to that.

Around one in every twenty-five photos was decent, by which I mean their features were clearly visible. But the rest? Were these guys actually aware of the impression they were creating by their profile picture? I mean, first impressions and all. Clearly not.

Some didn't even provide a photo at all. BIG mistake.

Well, left-swipe for all you, probably-married, on-the-prowl lovelies.

Other left-swipe contenders were all those photos of flowers, mountains, a bottle of beer, a beach, a heart, a teddy bear, a sports car or motor bike. Not today, I'm afraid, sweetheart. Or ever!

Another favourite was a profile photo of a kitten or a dog. Well, that's cute! Not.

Then again, there were those with sayings, quotes, poetry. Give me a break!

Another no-no: a photo of Richard Gere, Omar Sharif or Jason Statham, Sean Connery and, who was it? Oh, George Clooney. Really, George? Really?

If these guys thought that was a way of attracting Julia Roberts, Catherine Zeta Jones or Angelina Jolie lookalikes — well, my advice? Have a major rethink. Jeez!

And ninety-five per cent of the rest, who actually bothered to provide a photo of themselves, had not checked the photo before posting. Some were in the shade, some with their back to the camera, others in a motorbike helmet, or on a boat with their face hidden.

And the sunglasses! Oh, those shades! Certainly didn't inspire fifty shades of attraction in me. Most guys look undeniably cooler in shades, yet at the same time, they lose their individuality, joining the "Men in Black" brigade. A profile pic with shades is okay if you provide other pics without them, but in general, all the Men in Black went left.

The need for more specific filters just kept growing: something for the Tinder admin team to think about.

By the time my allotted hour was up, I had decided to right-swipe five. Three came back as a match. Result! I was excited. Was I brave enough to make the first move? Hell, yes. This part I could manage.

'*Buenos dias.*' That would do. About to leave the app, my interest had been piqued. Another five minutes.

Great decision. Two guys literally stopped me in my tracks. The first, a full-face photo, uninhibited, staring directly at you, like the Mona Lisa. A bit of a hippy look going on, grey hair blowing slightly in the breeze; beautiful, deep brown, magnetic eyes. On a yummy scale of one to ten, a definite eleven. I clicked for info and yes, he had provided a synopsis of what he was looking for and why, simply put, plus four more photos, revealing even more of him. Lived in Ibiza, but was retired, travelling around in his motorhome.

Without a second thought, I right-swiped him, crossing everything I'd got that he'd swipe me back.

No more than a minute later, I found myself staring at my Mum's idol dreamboat. Well not really, but he was a dead ringer for him. The guy who played Aristotle Onassis with Jacky Onassis— oh, what's his damned name? This is the thing about getting old. Anthony Quinn! Yes, that's him. Only us oldies will remember him, but oh boy, was he a hottie. And here I was, staring his double right in the face! He had a grey ponytail and a pensive pose, as if in conversation with someone. A really effective shot. I was impressed. The other few photos were equally good, plus he had included a little blurb about his passion for the theatre. And he lived in Granada, a mere fifty minutes away from me. Right-swipe: another eleven. Two in one day. Come on, guys. Swipe me back, why don't you?

CHAPTER 5
It's a Date!

Of course, the initial three matches were the first to chat: Alberto, Miguel, and Erik from Belgium.

Five minutes in, polite introductory exchange over, Erik calmly asked me if I was a true blonde, and did I have blonde pubes! Seriously?

I didn't waste a second.

'Erik, how perceptive of you,' I wrote. 'I have them professionally dyed every fortnight. Today they are a deep pink with a burgundy stripe down the centre.'

Before unmatching him, laughing out loud, I added 'Thank you for your interest.'

A potential pervert, if ever there was one. Further down the line, having chatted on the phone, had video calls, actually met and liked each other, then this would have been okay, I suppose. But after five minutes? Was this how it was going to be? I'd better buckle up for the ride then, I thought. Bring it on!

I know: I'll categorise them and then see if this online dating malarkey is worth the aggro it seems to be putting me through, I decided.

So we'll have Frogs, Fraudsters, Perverts and Princes. Perfect. Kicking off with a point for the Perverts.

Alberto restored my faith in mankind, simply by being polite, giving me a couple of compliments and not mentioning pubic hair. After fifteen minutes, I was ready for a break and he was fine with it. He lasted a couple of weeks, and from my side, we didn't move any further forward than that first chat. He was my first frog. Nothing actually wrong but after two weeks we were struggling to find stuff in common.

It's so true that you have to kiss a lot of frogs before you meet your prince. For the rest of the year, October to December 2019, I had umpteen chats with Frogs. Frogs come in all shapes and sizes. I put guys in the Frog column, not just for lack of spark, but for lots of other things. So, along with No-Spark Frog, there were quite a few other subcategories. I made thirteen, all unlucky for me.

1. No-Spark Frog.

2. No-Hope Frog. Not much ambition. Waits for the world to come to him, and watches it pass him by while waiting.

3. Dependent Frog. Lives with Mum. Yes! Fifty-five plus, there are still guys doing this. Not their mum living with them and their family, but in her house with her still doing their laundry, for God's sake. Of course, some Dependent Frogs think this is okay to the point of

being proud. Maybe I should rename him Sad Bastard Frog? Nah. Not worth the effort.

4. Fanatic Frog. Has a hobby that takes over half his life. More than a healthy, sociable interest. Could be anything from football or golf, to star-gazing, mountain climbing or online gaming.

5. Victim Frog. Mr. Sorry-for-himself. Woe is me; sees the glass as half empty. Makes excuses for his sad situation. Plays the blame game. Lives in the past, harbouring resentment. I must ask how to say 'Man up!' in Spanish. Or not. Victim Frog wouldn't have a clue what I was going on about, so no point.

6. Steady, Same-Old Frog. Lives in the same area he was born in, went to school, then work. Happy with his lot. All very admirable, but we would never get on and he would never get his head around my lifestyle.

7. Unromantic Frog. For me, that's like eating a cream cake with no cream. Enough said.

8. Shy Frog. Not much confidence. Indecisive. Feels uncomfortable laughing out loud.

9. Exclusive Frog. During the first five minutes, asks if I am chatting to any other guys and gets annoyed when I say of course! Hello?

10. Pink-Shirt Frog. Has a certain style that puts me off.

11. Poser Frog. Loves mentioning his height, weight, how much he trains at the gym, namedrops. Wants my number so he can send me yet more photos of his youthful looks and toned body.

12. Perfect Frog. Whatever the subject, he's been there, done that, got the T-shirt.

13. Chauvinist Frog. The three Ks from Hitler: Kinder, Küche, Kirche (kids, kitchen, church). A woman's place and all that.

I mean, we are on the site to find a relationship, which ultimately means we are looking for compatibility. The Frogs all seemed decent guys, but for whatever reason, not worth pursuing further for a romantic relationship with me. I mean, some of these guys could have been in two or three of the above categories, not just the one. Imagine going on a date with Pink-Shirt Poser Perfect!

My mobile informed me someone had sent me a rose on Tinder.

This must be number three, Miguel. Good start, I thought.

But no. There he was. The Anthony Quinn lookalike, starting a chat.

I warmed to him straightaway. He knew who he was, what he liked, seemed interested in me, there was a certain *chispa*, or spark, from the off. Just forty-five minutes away in Granada, retired yet extremely active with the life he had carved out for himself. So we could still retain our independence, but set "us" time aside whenever we wanted. Seems too good to be true, I thought.

We chatted for a few days and agreed to exchange mobile numbers so we could connect on WhatsApp and call each other. His voice was quite deep and at first, I was overcome with nerves in the effort to understand him. I needn't have worried: his second language was Italian and his English non-existent, so my level of Spanish was the best we had.

I got used to the tone of his voice after a few days and calmed down. And then, the following week, he sent THE message. Suggesting we meet. However, I had always imagined meeting someone for a coffee, for an hour or two, for the first time. And I could see he clearly had other ideas. The weather was holding up and he was going down to the coast to the beach on the Costa Tropicana for the day on Saturday. Would I care to accompany him?

My heart sank. I started texting my reply straight away.

- Of course I wouldn't! What do you think I am? Stupid? You might murder me!

And with that, I pressed send.

My trouble is, what you see is what you get. I am exactly what is says on the tin and my instinctive reactions are honest, but often abrupt. And anyway, apart from his worrying assumption that we had built up sufficient trust to go to the coast for a whole day together, for me the first date had to be closer to home. If I didn't like him, for whatever reason, I needed to be able to escape. I wasn't prepared to drive out of my safety zone all the way to Granada. No way, José.

He didn't reply. That was a Thursday. Seventy-eight questions were running through my head, with no answers. The film my mum had loved so much was The Greek Tycoon, 1978, where Anthony Quinn plays Aristotle Onassis and has a relationship with Jacky Kennedy. Much like the Dodi Fayed/Princess Diana theme, nearly two decades later. He had certainly captured Mum's interest. Now I'd lost the chance to see if the Spanish version would capture mine. Stopped before it even started. Ah well — another day, another date, I suppose.

I was wrong. Sunday evening, he sent a message, asking if I still wanted to meet and if so, where and when. Result! We arranged for him to drive up to my town on Tuesday and meet in the Park Bar at one o'clock. Finally, I had my first date. On my patch. On my terms. And with Anthony Quinn, my Spanish Tycoon, to boot.

CHAPTER 6
Santa Claus and Secret Spies

Although now mid-November, with much chillier days, it had yet to rain properly, as in cats and dogs, all day long, puddle rain. Yeah, you've guessed it. Tuesday was that day.

'You be careful, Mum,' Amira warned me. 'Sit in one of the outside-covered terraces, where there are lots of people around. More public than inside. And leave your phone on. I'm off to the gym. See you later.'

I hate brollies. More like lethal weapons. People all shapes and sizes plodding down a narrow pavement taking others' eyes out and whatever else along the way. Then, when you get to wherever you're going, you have to put it in an umbrella stand or risk water all over the floor. Of course, later, the rain stops and you stride out without the damned thing. So apart from being dangerous, they're pretty expensive, as you need to keep buying them over and again.

My alternative? Hats. Love 'em. I bundled myself up in boots, yellow coat and hat and drove the ten minutes to the Park Bar. Parking up, a message flashed onto my screen. He had arrived! Damn! No chance for me to choose where we'd sit. Hey ho.

I braved the rain and hurried into the bar. Clocked him straight away, at one end, with a coffee. He had left his hair down, which reached his shoulders. Glancing up as I approached, he stood up to greet me with a kiss on each cheek.

I was extremely nervous but pleasantly surprised. He looked just like his photos, and now I could see he was tall, too. I faffed about a bit with my hat and coat, while he ordered me a coffee, but we were soon installed, chatting away. He did most of the talking, and I focused intently on his face, wanting to understand properly. It took all my concentration.

So, imagine my surprise when the waiter came over with a bunch of artificial red roses, asking for 'Jacky?'

'Yes, that's me,' I told him, in dismay.

Crikey, a first date, and he buys me plastic flowers. Some of my initial illusions were being shattered as I let this all sink in.

But I was wrong.

'Here you are, *señora*,' the waiter continued, handing them over. 'There is a message, as well. These are from Carlos, who thanks you for one of the most amazing nights of his life last night.'

What the—? And all of this in Spanish, so *Señor* Quinn was all ears!

Could this actually be happening? I stood up to face the waiter, frowning directly into his eyes.

'Carlos? I don't know any Carlos. And I certainly didn't give him the time of his life last night! So why don't you go back to this Carlos and tell him exactly where he can shove these!'

I pushed the flowers back at him and sank miserably into my seat. This was a disaster, my worst nightmare. What was going on?

I realised the waiter hadn't moved. 'Sorry *señora*, but I don't know who Carlos is, either. He simply asked me to bring these over and left.'

'Well, good riddance!' I snapped. 'And as for these...' I snatched the offending bunch of plastic from him and rammed them into the little table bin, usually for serviettes. 'And that's the best place for them,' I muttered.

The waiter saw his chance and fled.

Snapping back into the present, I stared across the table to see my date's bemused features. Holy Moses, he's going to need some sort of explanation, or we are scuppered. Talk about first impressions! If he had any before, boy are they going to change after this.

I had — what — a few seconds at most to decide how to play this. I went for the truth.

'Well, that's the weirdest thing that's ever happened to me. And today of all days. Here. With you. At this table. And do you know what? I bet nothing like that will ever happen to me again in my lifetime. So where do we go from here?'

Antonio picked up the little table bin stuffed full of plastic and examined them.

'Well, I have to say, I find it bizarre. I mean, in Spain, to present a lady with a gift of plastic flowers is bad luck. Simply not done. So I think there is something else going on here.'

'Can we put it behind us and start over?'

I was feeling more than a little shell-shocked and at that point, ready to throw in the towel unless we could move past this.

He smiled. 'It was quite funny, on another level, don't you think?'

'Ask me tomorrow,' I replied, smiling right back at him.

A couple of minutes later, again engrossed in what he was saying, something made me look up. You know that feeling when someone is looking at you? Yes, that one.

I cast my eyes to the next table. A couple of women with black hats pulled down over their hair, were looking at me. As I looked at their faces, I got the shock of my life. My eyes widened, and any conversation was forgotten. There, on the next table were Amira and Becky, a friend. Kill me now!

I leaned over to touch Antonio on the sleeve. 'Can I stop you for a minute? I would like to introduce you to…' I swallowed and went for it. 'My daughter, Amira.'

For the second time that day — no, hang on — the second time in that half-hour, Antonio was thrown into my crazy world of weirdness. Not really understanding what was going on, he shook hands, greeted them both. Then, to add to this oh-so-perfect afternoon, Becky's husband appeared from the other end of the bar to say hello, as well. Jesus! After a couple of embarrassing moments, they all took their leave.

I decided to go with the flow.

'Look, she obviously wanted to check you out,' I smiled. 'Shall we call it a day?'

I was sure he would be aching to do a runner by this time. So I'd make it easy for him.

'Well, I'm hungry. Shall we find somewhere for lunch?'

We found a small Italian restaurant and managed a couple of hours of quality time together, away from prying eyes and other intrusions. Still pouring down when we left, he gave me a long hug and said he'd be in touch. I watched him fade into the dull day and went in search of my car.

***

I had had the foresight to put my phone on silent. I checked it to see no less than four messages from Amira.

- Have you left yet?
- You are taking too long.
- This is far too long for a first date.
- Come home.'

Kids!

Turns out, Amira never went to the gym at all. She and Becky had raided the Chinese shop (the equivalent of Poundworld) for hats and plastic flowers. They installed her husband inside the bar with his newspaper, out of the rain. Approaching the bar, they asked the waiter if he would present the flowers to a blonde lady in a yellow coat and hat when she arrived, with a message from the infamous Carlos. Everything prepped, they then went to sit on the covered terrace outside and wait for me. But when Antonio arrived first and disappeared inside the bar, they were stumped, because with all the rain, the tables were all occupied inside.

They watched the whole set up from a distance, laughing their socks off. And as soon as a table became available, they were in there, looking at us first hand. Little devils!

'You surely can't fancy him, Mum,' was Amira's helpful observation. 'He looks just like Santa Claus, for God's sake!'

Ahh, the younger generation has missed out on so much, the seductive allure of a certain Anthony Quinn included. Reduced from my Spanish tycoon to Santa Claus in a heartbeat, without a second thought.

He messaged me when he arrived home and said he'd chuckled quite a bit at the prank and was, in fact, quite impressed at how my daughter wanted me to be safe.

It could so easily have gone the other way. But then, if he couldn't see the funny side, when I was able to, he wasn't the guy for me. He said he hoped our meeting was the first of many and sent a kiss. Well, I know I joke around with my friends, telling them how I lurch from one disaster to another: that day sort of said it all.

Before sleeping, a notification of a new match came through. OMG, Ibiza man. He simply stated he was travelling to South America for two weeks and would be in touch on his return. So that would be the first week of December. I made a mental note.

CHAPTER 7
Would YOU Pay for It?

Up to this point, I had used Tinder for free, but of course, it's a business and they're in it to make a profit. The free part must be the sweetener, the enticer, to seduce you into paying for… what exactly?

Clicking through men's photos on Tinder, a page popped up regularly for 'Tinder Gold', apparently giving you access to their idea of 'la crème de la crème' for a monthly subscription. Sometimes they even sent you a link to chat to one guy of your choice, as extra enticement.

I was being enticed quite enough, thank you, so I never went there. But they were persistent, I'll give them that. Every time a Gold member right-swiped you, Tinder messaged to say I had lost a match. So you think you've missed out. When actually, you haven't.

The thing is, I hadn't gone out of my way to advertise my Tinder exploits with my friends. I mean, although growing in popularity, even among the older generation, it's not something you just come straight out with and talk about.

Curious, I took the bull by the horns one day, chatting with friends, and casually threw in a question.

'Don't suppose any of you have ever tried online dating, have you?'

'I have,' piped up Orla. 'POF'.

'Hello, what?'

'"Plenty Of Fish." Online dating.'

This was news to me. I actually laughed out loud. What a name! Loved it already. I decided to investigate, try a few of these apps, compare the experiences and see where they were all coming from.

So I became a free member of POF, Badoo and Meetic. The differences were clear. Tinder seemed to be the king of them all, with millions of members. So as members, with so much choice, they have the monopoly on controlling the subscription methods. It's quick: you simply provide a photo, a short description and away you go. Get swiping.

The advantage of Tinder, which I hadn't realised until looking at other apps, is that you can chat only to your matches. So you aren't snowed under with messages from all and sundry.

This is huge. A massive sifting out from the off. And free. Another plus is that if you then change your mind, you simply unmatch them. Sorted. With other apps, they stay there, creating an annoyingly useless never-ending contact list.

I can't be the only person to notice this. On Badoo and POF, I had so many Frogs hanging around and there wasn't much I could do about it. In this aspect, Tinder, with its quick and simple philosophy, wins hands down.

I suppose it was inevitable that as their popularity rose, Tinder would restrict the free option. And indeed they did. Their most recent update places daily limits on how many likes free users can use per day. Unlimited likes now set you back a tenner a month.

What premium features does Tinder offer?
- Rewind — Undo your last Like
- Super Like — Express extra interest in someone by tapping the blue star and your profile will be highlighted in blue for them
- Boost — Get bumped to the top of people's Discovery queue for thirty minutes, for more immediate matches
- Passport — search for matches anywhere
- Likes You — a list of who likes you
- Top Picks — member profiles tailored to you based on what you have in common.

In a nutshell, all messages are free, it's user-friendly and anyone can use it. Most online dating sites require you to be a paid member to send and receive text messages. Although you can only message people you have matched with, this is one of the online dating options that allows you to interact with other people without paying for a subscription. Plus, Tinder has a few safety features that users can take advantage of, such as:

- Photo Verification — Verify your profile by copying a selfie pose. The photo is verified by human and facial recognition technology.

Not so much with the competition.

Let's consider POF. Okay, messaging is free. A good start. Other online dating sites allow users to sign up for free and then charge them to look at other profiles or send messages. While POF does offer a subscription, all major features are entirely free. You can message as many people as you want, search profiles and create a profile entirely for free. Plenty of Fish states that the site's most popular features are completely free and always will be.

Then you can block another member or report the user for their behaviour. The POF team will carefully investigate their account for suspicious activity. All reports are strictly confidential.

But the app doesn't allow you to send photos. So if you get chatting and want to progress it with up-to-date photos, you have to give out your phone number and do it via WhatsApp.

To get more views, likes, swipes and taps on their profile, members have to purchase a paid membership, credits, tokens, or coins. If you pay, you get the following extra features:
- Upload sixteen pictures to a dating profile
- Unlock every user's Extended Profile
- See if your emails were read or deleted

- Show up first on Meet Me!
- Experience POF without any ads
- Find out the date and time someone viewed your profile
- See who viewed your profile
- Send three virtual gifts per day
- Stand out amongst all searches
- Get access to the Username Search feature.

I then tried Badoo. Yes, Badoo offers a free app and the option to create a free profile. You can start chatting with other members free of charge.

If you pay for it, you get the following:

- Liked You — users can see who voted "Yes" on their profile in Encounters
- Invisible Mode — members can browse Badoo without anyone seeing
- Undo Your Last Vote — be able to undo your "No" votes in Encounters
- Added You As A Favourite — members can see who likes them the most
- Chat To Popular Users — access to the most popular people on Badoo
- First To Contact New People — chat with new members as soon as they join
- Highlight Your Message — members' messages will be read first by their contacts
- Stickers — access to cool stickers

- In order to create a Badoo profile, users must upload a picture of themselves posing in a specific way. Badoo matches this photo with your uploaded profile pictures. Each profile picture goes through a quick verification process. This helps stop scammers and fake accounts from being made.

Another positive aspect is the simplicity of the app itself: it's easy to sign up for and get started. This seems to be their philosophy. You can get started, which roughly translates as basic in the extreme. Not a lot for nothing there.

To get the most out of the app, you probably have to consider buying credits or paying for a premium account to access the site's premium features.

And on to Meetic.

You can register for free, but again, to be able to enjoy the site's premium features, you must pay for one of their monthly subscriptions. And if you decide to pay? They are not cheap. Thirty-five euros a month to be precise. One of the fun features of Meetic is being able to "wink" at someone you like and receive a wink back. Another is that the site sends notifications via email for you to be updated all the time.

However, if you plan to utilise the site without a subscription, prepare yourself for a little disappointment. Free is so basic, it's frustrating. You can barely get past first base! Literally, to be able to answer messages, you need to subscribe. And this was my main bugbear. If you decide you like someone and they are a Premium Member, you cannot message them. Hello? To me, this is not good. Not good at all. From either side. Some poor guy paying for it and the girl of his dreams picks him, but they can't hook up just because she isn't paying? Lose-lose.

I saw a potential hottie, clicked on "message", and was told, "Subscribe to be able to message this guy." Come on! This is mean! You've already whetted my appetite and I can't take a bite? Well, I for one didn't fall for it. And the reason is this: Tinder, POF and Badoo, just three of the competition, all offer free messaging. I therefore bowed gracefully out of Meetic and turned my attention instead to the other three.

It's a fact these days that this is a fast-growing industry, and like any other, there will be companies under the same umbrella yet with different approaches. You need to decide what you're in it for and if you would really benefit from the premium features on offer. Or if you just test the waters, chatting initially for free. I ended up having a right old time opting for the free route. And believe me, I wouldn't have had it any other way.

At this precise point in time, what are your thoughts on the subject? Would you be persuaded to take advantage of the perks on offer by subscribing? A hell of a lot of people are. The sites bank on it. You get a taster and then think, this could be fun. Okay, in for a penny... The question remains, would you pay for it?

CHAPTER 8
Ripples in a Perfect Puddle

¡Buenos días guapissima! A rose and two kisses followed.

I stared at the message in surprise. A morning message, and one so— well, directly suggestive. I mean, 'Good morning, beautiful' wasn't exactly his style. To date, he had been chatty, polite, sociable, forgiving, but not exactly romantic or overly interested in me. My Spanish tycoon, Antonio, aka Anthony Quinn, had leapt into previously untested waters with me, especially with the rose and kisses.

So he's interested and letting me know. Well, that's okay by me, I thought. Let's see where this goes.

'Morning. You're up early,' I wrote, not playing the romantic card yet.

'Are you free this coming Saturday?' was his reply.

He wanted to show me a few hidden jewels of the city, on foot, that were not on any tourist trail. Right up my alley. I agreed to drive to Granada that Saturday, late morning.

***

It was cold. But dry. Jeans, trainers, yellow coat. Ready. We met in a bar he told me about, where there was plenty of parking. We had a coffee, left my car and went in his up near the ramparts at the rear of the great Alhambra palace and fortress.

Over the following three hours or so, he led me on a tapas trail, up twisty windy streets, through markets, a square for artists, the bohemian quarter and the old flamenco haunts. We had a beer in one of these, a teeny tiny bar famous for flamenco, another crammed with posters and pictures of local bullfighters. He introduced me to the owners, both establishments in the family for generations, and told me a little about each.

I was really enjoying the whole experience. The knot in the base of my stomach since the coffee in that first bar had just about dissolved. As we left the bullfighter bar, he gently reached down, took my hand and we strolled on, more like teenagers, hand in hand. I was being super polite, on my best behaviour, if a bit uptight worrying constantly about my Spanish.

Then he took me to one of the oldest bars in Granada, *Bar Aliator, Los Caracoles* (snails), renowned, of course, for its snails and packed with Spanish locals, even out of season. We sat in the square and Antonio disappeared inside, presumably to the toilet. He wasn't long and a few minutes later, they brought out drinks accompanied by a bowl of snails, which normally I would boke at. But this was NOT the time to be squeamish.

'For you! Enjoy!' he beamed at me.

A vegetarian, my Anthony Quinn had actually gone to the incredibly gentlemanly effort of ordering me the specialty as a treat, a gesture. That panicky fluttering in my stomach started its familiar churning as I stared down at the dish, a smile glued with Solvite on my face.

How was I going to get over this? Was it possible to eat one without throwing up? The little voice of reason was whispering in my ear.

Come on, girlie. You're not stupid. You think downing one will be enough? Think again. You'll have to finish off the whole bowl, as he doesn't eat them. Get your head around that one!

An unexpected dilemma, creating ripples in my so-far perfect puddle.

I looked around desperately for a bin, tree, plant, anything to gradually dispose of the slimy little beasts undetected. *Nada*. That's the thing about Spanish cities. Loads of bins. Everywhere. Except when your life depends on it.

I took another glance in the bowl. Yep, must be around twenty-five or so, almost floating bulbously in the orange *salsa mediterranea*, almost as if the damned things were sunbathing.

At that precise moment, a guitarist broke the momentum and wove his magic, strumming flamenco, while another guy clapped and stomped the traditional dance and a young slip of a girl with a surprisingly strong, deep voice sang her heart out. They shattered the peace of the afternoon and the dulcet tones of different conversations, yet it was a welcome interruption, well-received by the punters, changing the ambiance from tranquil to vibrant in an instant.

They were on the opposite pavement, behind Antonio. A desperate plan was forming, madly rushing around my head, and as he turned to enjoy the performance, I whispered a silent prayer, went for it and reached into that dreaded bowl. Not two or three — a whole handful. Straight into my coat pocket.

This wonderful, perfectly executed plan lasted precisely three seconds from start to finish. Except that it wasn't. Neither wonderful nor perfectly executed. Not one of my best at all, in fact, as I stared in horror at the watery orange salsa still dripping between my fingers.

Oh my God! What was I thinking?

I came out of panic mode to realise he was still watching the music and I had more time. Fumbling in my bag, I fished out a pack of tissues, stuffed one in my pocket and tried to wrap as many orange-coated snails as possible into it, to stop them staining the coat and absorb some of the liquid. This done, I hurriedly pushed another tissue under the original one and topped the whole lot off with a third on the top, so that it protruded slightly. I wiped my hand down and only then breathed out. Phew! That would have to do.

My *coup de grace* was taking the toothpick provided, spearing a couple, sitting back in the chair and trying to stop my heart from bursting out of my chest.

He turned, said something complimentary about the music and surveyed the snail scene.

My heart stopped.

'Ha! You like them! I told you! Shall we order another bowl?'

It was all I could do to escape to the bathroom, flush the damned things down the loo and get us both out of there.

All I could think of was thank the Lord my coat is yellow. It would have been a different story with white beige or light blue.

By now, he was on a high and I was exhausted. He said we could go back to his place, he would cook and I drive home the following day. I knew he wouldn't push me to jump into bed. Besides, I had him down as a true gent. So I agreed.

His flat was bang in the city centre, three bed, two bath, first floor. Of course, at sixty-five, he had his routines, and one of them was to get out of his outdoor clothes when he was at home. He changed and brought me his slippers and a pair of tartan pyjama bottoms. Hey ho, here we go.

'Sorry,' he shrugged. 'It's all I have. You'll have to turn the bottoms up and these are my only slippers.'

In the end, we compromised. He kept the slippers. I had my socks and wore his PJ tartan bottoms, turned up. He gave me the grand tour of his bachelor pad, where he'd made the second bedroom into his office.

The bathroom was the size of a cupboard with a solitary toothbrush in a glass on the sink.

Shit! Toothbrush, I thought.

I followed him back into the living area, where he put the TV on for me while he busied himself in the kitchen rustling up something for us to eat.

This gave me time to think. It had been rash, I saw, to agree to stay over. I had nothing for the morning, no toothbrush, no face, as in creams, makeup, a hairbrush. My early morning natural look with no makeup remover is a sight to behold; one I reserve exclusively for the bathroom mirror.

Hell's teeth! I had got away with the snail trail by the skin of my teeth and walked straight into another dilemma. And there didn't seem to be any way around it. This relationship was doomed.

And what was worse, I had to spend the whole night with him, fully aware it wouldn't last another twenty-four hours. As he didn't have any tea, my all-time lifesaver, I got a glass of water and gave myself a pep talk.

Let's make the last evening exciting, fun and one to remember. Tomorrow is another day.

Dinner was okay, I guess, if a bit sterile. He was friendly and polite, but obviously not used to entertaining. As he didn't drink after four p.m., he didn't offer me one. I'm not referring to alcohol, although I would have really welcomed a glass of red at that point.

No, any drink other than water. I drink copious cups of tea and coffee, so I found this slightly uncomfortable.

Then he wanted to wash up himself, not letting me in the kitchen. And when I took a book down, he quietly took it from my hands and put it back on the shelf.

But that was it, I realised. He was who he was. Methodical and liked things in their place. Nothing wrong with that. He had lived alone for a few years now.

'What do you think of the artwork?' was his opener after dinner on the sofa.

He could have said anything personal, asked me anything. It was, after all, an intimate situation if we chose it to be. Instead, it was turning out to be rather awkward. We didn't laugh much. I was nervous and he was serious. No room for a spark or sexual attraction. It was driving me mad.

I'll have to kiss him and find out, I thought.

So I did. He was explaining one of his paintings to me, standing by it, waving an arm around. I jumped off the sofa, took his arm, slid my other around his back, and on my tiptoes drew him gently towards me. It took him by surprise but he didn't complain. We kissed. I caressed his neck. He pressed his lips to mine, holding me tightly.

Well guys, that was the deal-breaker. I don't want to diss him down but let's just say that two-out-of-ten was being kind. The vibe was so not there, I didn't even close my eyes. So either he was out of practice or didn't fancy me. Frog: one, Prince Charming: nil. Bummer.

I pulled away with a smile, stuck the night out and went to bed early. At least he found another toothbrush, so not all bad. When I awoke the following morning, he was up making coffee! So he does drink coffee, but obviously only in the morning. He had things to do, so straight after that, he dropped me at my car with just a casual goodbye.

I let him down a few days later and he was, as always, a gentleman and understanding. Probably relieved. No happy-ever-after for us. Sealed with a kiss? More like crucified.

I realised, if it's not going well, get out. Stop wasting time. I don't owe these guys anything. Well, other than honesty and doing it in a kind way. Same with the texting. It's okay to just not reply, or stop messaging. You don't have to justify anything. It's something I got better at, the more I did it.

And that's another major difference between actual and online dating. You meet tons of people online, so naturally there are going to be tons of times you get bored, or just don't want to chat any more because he's crazy about stamp collecting or Star Wars. In real life, you may only meet three or four people in a year. It's a totally different ballgame; one which we all need to get our heads around, play by the rules and come up smelling of roses.

In the meantime, Ibiza man got back in touch. He was really easy to chat to and my heart did a little flip every time I saw a message from him. Returned from his travels, he was back on his home ground. His tenants were moving out of his house in Ibiza and he was repainting, doing it up a bit for the new arrivals.

After a week of chatting via the dating site, we exchanged numbers. He called to speak once a week and boy, his voice. Every bit as gorgeous as his photo, and his laugh was infectious. We just seemed to forget time. He was clear from the outset: he was looking for someone to share his trips with, nothing serious. Well, that suited me. A couple of trips a year to far-flung places off the beaten track. Hell, yes to that. And my independence for the rest of the year. Count me in.

Christmas came and went and we all looked forward to the new year, a new decade. 2020. I decided to look at my checklist and see if a pattern was emerging. An end-of-year inventory of my online dating experiences. It was just scribbled on a blank page in the back of my 2019 diary. And in fact, it was encouraging. Thirty-seven Frogs, two potential Prince Charmings, two Perverts and not a single Fraudster. Not bad at all. I must be doing something right. On the right track at any rate.

I remember raising a glass, and in line with Spanish tradition, stuffing twelve grapes into my mouth to be consumed before the last chime of midnight and hoping for a fresh start, a bright future ahead of me, the best year ever, in fact.

Well, what a joke that turned out to be.

CHAPTER 9
The Big Bad Wolf: Covid-19

'I'll huff and I'll puff and I'll blow your world down.'

And that pretty much says it all. When news of a virus in Wuhan City, China was first broadcast on TV in the UK, it was a brief announcement, followed by a report on a robbery and the football league tables. The weather forecast must have captured more attention. That oh-so-familiar, shameful attitude, which Joe public reveals so often. You know the one. Watches a documentary about drought and starvation in Africa, glued to the screen because Angelina Jolie is there. Had she not been an ambassador for the cause, he wouldn't have bothered to watch the programme at all. Feeling a false sense of pity, not sending a donation, then going out to McDonald's and buying a lottery ticket. The not-on-my-patch brigade. The country is full of them. The stragglers with a social conscience don't have a hope of educating Joe. Pointless. He might hear your words, but he's not listening. Not, that is, until you bring the wolf to his front door.

Which is how Big Bad Covid-19 snuck in. Right to our doors. With a huff and a puff.

Covid-19: appropriately named as it first raised its terrifying head in December 2019 in China. The enormity of what was happening did not dawn on the Western world until weeks later. Across Europe and the USA, we were celebrating Thanksgiving, Christmas, New Year, partying our hearts out, going to concerts, restaurants and sports events, hugging and kissing at every opportunity, shopping 'til we dropped.

> This is the way the world ends
> This is the way the world ends
> This is the way the world ends
> Not with a bang but a whimper.

T.S. Eliot *"The Hollow Men"*

The realisation that the virus had not been contained was like T.S. Eliot's poem. It hit, not with a bang, but a whimper. Like ink slowly spreading across blotting paper. Black ink seeping into fresh, white blotting paper. Horrifying in its reality, its darkness, its power.

***

Blissfully ignorant, unaware of what was just around the corner, life went on as normal. José (Ibiza man) and I had our first video call and somehow that made all the difference. It shifted the whole relationship up a notch. He was just what it said on the tin. We got on like a house on fire. He showed me around his house and the painting he was doing. He reckoned another month and he would be ready to come back to mainland Spain, spending a few days in Alicante before coming to meet me. If we got on well, he could stay for up to two weeks, he said. He wanted to make me a special spicy mushroom soup, a recipe from his grandmother. We could plan future trips for the rest of the year, he said. He fancied Morocco and I was leaning towards Greece. So we compromised and agreed to do both, lol. Boy things were certainly hotting-up. Stomach-churning stuff, and this time, thankfully, nothing to do with snails.

By now I was chatting to quite a few Romeos. Ben, a doctor for the UN, from Spain but on a contract in Iran; Frank, an American, out on an oil rig; Miguel, poet and philosopher, an hour's drive away; Jonathan, retired in Huelva; Tim, an engineer in Malaga; Joel, a farmer in France; Peter, a business man in Holland; Pierre, an estate agent in Marbella; Santi, retired in Roquetas; Gordon, artist in Mijas; Dean, a musician in Jaen; Derek, newly arrived in Spain. As yet unclassified: none of them Frogs. Yet.

Time would tell.

Indeed, as time went by, as with anything I suppose, Tindering became easier to handle. I relaxed. Big mistake.

Originally, I had made a plan with four simple guidelines. The first two, to enjoy and put aside time for it, seemed to be going well, the reason for the rise in my self-confidence. But I was falling way short of the other two: being careful of information I gave out and meeting them asap.

I mean, what was the point of chatting for weeks and finally meeting up to spend an excruciatingly boring couple of hours in their company? Or was it better to take the time needed to get to know them quite well and then decide if it was worth meeting up? What worked better for me, I decided, was to meet as soon as possible.

Over the next six weeks or so, I did just that. First, I contacted Derek for a meet. Our common interest was 1970's music: Pink Floyd, Genesis, Led Zeppelin, David Bowie. He was new to Spain, living in a mobile home, looking to buy. As the drive was quite a few hours, and Amira was with me, I offered him the spare room and he drove over.

Well, let's just say that there's a first and last time for everything. He was charming, happy, chatty, obviously interested in me.

But.

That infamous, wonderful little word that covers a world of doubt, of can't-put-your-finger-on-it, of something's missing.

Yep, there was a but from the off. I felt it after five minutes. But I'd invited the guy to stay. It was nothing short of painful. He must have got the vibe. We went out to a couple of bars, then back home and I went up to bed quite soon after. The following morning, he surfaced and instead of taking the hint and leaving there and then, accepted the offer of breakfast, stretched it out to three coffees and two hours.

Awkward barely covered it. And I had no one to blame but myself. As Amira quite rightly stated, after he'd left, 'Mum, what were you thinking!'

We just burst out laughing. And in that moment, I moved a little further up the learning curve of this fascinating experience. Later, I was to have the same invite extended to me, several times over. Sounds great on the surface.

'If you want a drink, no problem. I have a spare room.'

Truth be told, it sure isn't. Great, that is. Thanks to my "Derek" experience, I moved another notch up the learning curve. I must politely decline every time. Lesson learned.

It was clear that it wasn't physically possible to meet all these PPs (Potential Princes), due to their circumstances.

I was quite drawn to Ben, the doctor for the UN, for instance. His two photos were dashing, quite the Mr. Darcy. We chatted easily via messaging but his contract didn't finish until August, he told me, so we would have to wait to meet up. But he messaged me each and every morning without fail and again during the day and he was extremely romantic. He worked long hours and was younger than me.

The same with Frank on the rigs. He looked great on his pictures, rugged and a certain something, a *'je ne sais quoi'*. His contract finished in November — light years away.

Then Bob from the States, also on a ship on a seven-month contract. He was a pretty boy, a few tattoos, six-pack, but came across as a teddy bear, not at all into himself, quite modest in fact. We laughed from the first conversation and to be honest, there wasn't anything not to like. Another one to wait for.

Crikey, I would have to be careful they didn't all finish their contracts in the same week. Some juggling challenge that would be, to be sure! You know what they say: you wait half an hour for a bus and then three come along all at once.

Joel, my French farmer, wasn't on the other side of the world on a ship or an oil rig. He lived in the south of France, worked the land, sold his products, rode his horses, sailed his boat. He worked hard every summer and took time off during the winter. He said he'd pay for my flight if I would agree to go for the weekend. He sent me videos of just about every damned breath he took. Talk about a video diary. I reserved his messages for reading on the loo! Although he made me laugh, and we shared video calls, I wasn't confident enough to jump on a plane to Perpignan for a whole weekend.

After a month, however, the decision was made for me. The tone of his videos shifted. They became intimate to the point of embarrassment. Something to do with being French? No idea. Had we both reached this point together and been comfortable with where we were in the relationship, then fine. But he suddenly started videoing himself in bed, with a running commentary. I'm quite sure you can imagine. Maybe he got fed up of singing in his van and progressed to the shower. Neither romantic, considerate nor my cup of tea. It all sort of descended from romance, suggestion and seduction to sex, rock-and-roll baby, let's let it all hang out! And in an instant. Overnight. Like I had turned a page and fallen all the way down to base level.

When he got a ruler out, he sealed his fate. I never watched to the end. But at least I learnt what a helicopter was. You'll have to Google that one, 'cos I am not writing it down, that's for certain!

He didn't qualify for the Pervert category, I decided. Admittedly, he made me shudder a little when I thought of how he had moved everything on, but that was his thing, not mine. A Frog for sure.

***

Okay then, how am I going to go about this? Scrolling through the list of contacts, I needed a definitive plan of action.

So let's start with the nearest and work through that way, I decided.

The nearest was Miguel. Retired, into philosophy and poetry, a soft, intense voice but clear enough to understand. Lived just outside Granada. We had only messaged, voice-mailed and called up to this point. No videos. He read his poetry over the phone with such passion that I was completely drawn into his world. Then he wrote not one, but two incredibly romantic poems for me and read them to me. I was hooked, enthralled. He didn't drone on with inane disjointed thoughts and archaic phrases. His style was short, direct, but meaningful in the extreme and he hit the spot. It was so romantic it felt sexual, but if you asked me to explain that, I wouldn't know where to start. He had a calm aura yet a burning passion inside, of which he had allowed me a tiny peek. A white-haired gent, no mistake.

I had work one morning in Granada, so agreed to meet him in Plaza de Gracia in the centre afterwards, around lunchtime. I arrived first and, not wanting to decide between the bars, sat on a bench. It was quite warm for winter, no wind and still sunny. He arrived soon after, two kisses in greeting and guided me to the terrace he obviously preferred.

We ordered tapas and sat there. And sat there. For an articulate, eloquent, talented guy on paper, he sure as hell was rubbish at small talk. Normally, I don't have a problem socialising, but this one was hard work. He smiled a lot, nodded, one-word answers, not asking me anything. So I didn't tell him anything. One rule of thumb: don't give anything away unless asked. Otherwise, you're just feeding your own ego. They ask, you respond, you connect. Or not. Simplifies things considerably.

When the tapas arrived, they sat there, untouched. In the end, I started, offered him one, to which he waved his hand and said, 'Later.'

Later? Later? I could have eaten a horse.

Plus, Miguel was the perfect example of NOT being what it said on the tin. He had turned up with old baggy jeans, about four sizes too big for him, held together with an old belt, a tatty long-sleeved T-shirt, a crimplene jacket and a scarf. As I had been working, I was wearing heels, a smart skirt-suit, coat, scarf, hat; formal, if you like. But it seemed like he had not made any effort to look good for a first date with the woman he had seduced so easily over the phone. He looked dishevelled and not that clean, to be honest. I mean, even without my work, I would have tried to look my casual best for any date. It was off-putting.

Then the gazing. He sat and gazed at me. The uncomfortable vibe was overriding any other experience, even my gnawing hunger. Whatever I tried, he just would not engage.

I bore it for thirty-five interminably awkward minutes. I know this, as I kept a keen eye on the clock. And then I lost it. Snapped. Not screamy, demonstrative, protesting snapping, but hellfire, just as powerful. A great example of when less is oh, so much more. I got up, said that I had a couple of hours more work, smiled directly into his eyes, thanked him for the tapas, and calmly walked away, at a normal pace, leaving him to ponder on his charm appeal and scrabble around for change to pay the bill.

***

Over the next couple of days, he messaged me. He thought I was stunningly beautiful. I had knocked his socks off. He couldn't stop staring into my eyes as deep as the ocean. How he would close his eyes and imagine looking deep into mine and he would be inspired to write another poem. And so on.

Yawn.

So he liked me. I mean, fair play, the guy knew how to wax lyrical, there's no denying it. But face to face — a nightmare, a complete disaster. Winner of The Samaritans' Employee of the Year, without a shadow of a doubt, where you help people without actually meeting them.

Initially, I didn't reply. Blocking him wasn't the way for me. I figured he deserved a response but wasn't sure which way to play it. In the end, I plumped for the truth. Ish. A Dear John message. Not harsh, just along the lines of how conversation didn't really flow, he didn't seem to be that interested, not asking me anything, not enjoying the food or surroundings. I even hinted that I was a little surprised at his choice of clothes for a first date. I said for my part there was no more mileage in the relationship and I wished him the best.

He changed his tune then. No more Mr Nice Guy. How could I do this after so long? All the days of messages, creativity oozing out of him, leading up to the first date. Oh yes, that was it. I was a "prick teaser". He told me to f*** off and sent me, by way of a parting gift, a photo of… go on, I'll give you three guesses. I kid you not: his wardrobe! I swear on Mum's grave. Fifty-plus shirts hanging neatly, all in a row, all the trousers hanging below.

Leaving him no excuse for his tramp look. The irony of that.

Category: Frog.

Lesson learned there was this: if the date isn't going well, you can just leave. You are under no obligation to stick it out, suck it up, bored out of your mind, or uncomfortable. And there's no unearthly reason to feel remotely guilty about it.

The why is simple. You have better things to do. The how is completely up to you. Is it just dragging on and you're not attracted to him in the slightest? Make up a believable excuse and leave. An early start, dinner to prepare, grandson to pick up.

Is he being too full-on, planning the next ten years together? Just say you're going to the bathroom and leave the back way. No point in thinking up excuses: he'll only want to go with you.

Is he being an arrogant arsehole? Then give him a bit of his own back.

'Well, it's been a joy, but I need to rush back and hang out the washing.'

Yep, maybe not in that very instant, but further down the line the penny will eventually drop that this activity is more riveting than listening to him.

Lots of Frogs. Not the time to give up in despair. My knight in shining armour must be out there somewhere. No, I would press on. Gordon, the artist, in Mijas was next. I had actually never been there and heard such great things about it, so after chatting for a couple of weeks, I agreed to drive down if he made lunch. The deal was struck

And then the world stopped being the world as we knew it.

CHAPTER 10
Lockdown

It was 30th January, 2020. The World Health Organisation (WHO) announced a global state of emergency, due to the virus.

During the first week of February, awareness of the coronavirus was planted firmly in our path with cases reported in Iran, South Korea and then Italy. It had reached Europe. Two Chinese tourists had visited Italy and were carriers. That's all it took. Oh my, how scary is that reality?

On 19th February, two thousand five hundred Valencia soccer fans mixed with forty thousand Atlanta supporters in Italy for a Champions League game in Milan, later described as "the bomb" which exploded the virus. The Big Bad Wolf was at our door.

With a huff here and a puff there, it spread alarmingly quickly. The news channels were all over it, raising awareness globally. And in response, the arrogance of nations shocked me to the core.

Donald Trump, the then-President of the USA immediately played the blame game: 'I blame the WHO.' And that was his valuable contribution to his country. Stick the bloody problem under the carpet and wait for it to go away. He had named and shamed. Job done. Next!

Boris Johnson ran away to Chequers, his country resort, for the entire parliamentary recess, out of sight in denial, his head in the sand. He missed five consecutive emergency meetings in the build-up to the coronavirus crisis and was called "missing in action" during the crucial weeks when the virus first arrived in the UK.

By mid-March, over eighty nations had reported the outbreak, and the WHO declared a pandemic on March 11th, 2020.

Meanwhile, I set off to meet artist, Gordon. He was friendly, hospitable, and I rode pillion for the first time ever, down to the port, where we had an Indian meal and a stroll along the seafront. Time passed quickly and after two glasses of wine, it would have been foolish to think about driving. The realisation that I was facing the night under this guy's roof began to dawn on me.

You stupid, stupid idiot! I told myself. Did the Derek experience teach you nothing? Well, make this the last time. Ever.

Back at the house, Gordon produced an open bottle of red, half full. I took a glass from him and accepted the offer of a spare room. Decision made.

I got away with it. Firstly, yes, there actually was a spare room, and secondly, my nerves made things crystal clear that sex was off the evening's agenda. He leaned in, I leaned out. He sat closer, I went to the loo. I was so totally out of my comfort zone and not a clue how to deal with any of it. I managed half a glass, said goodnight and went to bed, leaving him, most likely wondering what the hell had just happened.

Propping myself up on the pillows, I stared across the room at my reflection in the wardrobe mirror doors.

What is wrong with you? He is obviously interested. Why do you feel like rushing out right now and going home?

Which is exactly what I did the following morning when he brought me a cuppa and sat on the bed beside me while I drank it.

**

There's no logic to attraction. Gordon seemed to have it all. A quiet, amenable guy, obviously talented, happy with his lot. I would choose to have him as a neighbour without a second thought, but romantically, he didn't tick a single box. And there wasn't a thing I could do to change that.

Now rapidly becoming a master of extrication, I grabbed a shower, turned down breakfast on the seafront to drive home for an imaginary appointment. Suddenly, I couldn't wait to get out of there.

You know, you had a lucky break, I told myself on the way home. All you knew about him was what he'd told you on WhatsApp. And you drive an hour and a half to his *house,* his personal territory, relax, have a couple of drinks so your only option was to stay over? Why was this only occurring to me now? I had taken a huge personal risk, one which could have gone horribly wrong. Lesson learned. Do not go to a guy's house for the first date. Ever again. I might not be so lucky next time around.

Ben, the UN doctor, was still in the picture, as was Frank on the oil rig and Bob on a ship in the USA. A couple of messages from each every day, all of them hotting up a bit as the weeks passed.

Yet still, it was Ibiza man who I thought about, whose morning message I waited for, whose call made my week, whose smile made me melt. Soon we would meet face to face, when he came over for a week or two, depending on how we got on. I would imagine that moment, after so many months, when we actually set eyes on each other, how I would react, feel, if I would go into shy mode or throw my arms around him. I would play the scenario over and over. This was a guy ticking all of my boxes. So far.

Ben was becoming more amorous in his messages, yet didn't really ask me about me. He was attentive, polite, really fit in his photos, but from my end, I wasn't feeling a spark. Yet.

Frank wanted me to chat on Google Hangouts. Said it was easier on the oil rigs. So I obliged. He went for the friend approach, rather than showering me with compliments like Ben.

Bob, on the ship somewhere offshore in the USA, was focused mainly on his son, living with his parents in Spain. He wanted to take me to meet them all, he said, when his contract ended. I let it ride. It all seemed a bit far off for me. Plus, the fact that his son was only twelve, so if he turned out to be my Prince Charming, I would have to take that into account, as well.

I suppose we were all hoping Covid would fade away like a fluke storm. Instead, the government imposed social distancing and we were advised to wear masks in public places. The gym, where I swam thirty lengths every morning, closed its doors, along with many other "non-essential" businesses.

On March 14th, 2020, Pedro Sanchez declared a national lockdown for six weeks.

Amira and I had each other's company, at least. Apart from essentials, we were not allowed out. Not even for a walk. It was hard. Drastic. Necessary. Made a huge impact on us both.

After the initial couple of weeks of frustration, worry, stress and bickering, sometimes to the point of sitting in separate rooms, we gradually learned to adapt. Facetiming family and friends for one. Exercising with YouTube for another. Lots of series on Netflix. Each week, I donned a mask for the supermarket trip. Only one person allowed in the car. Frequent police checks.

Every evening at eight pm on the dot, the villagers went out onto their balconies to await the music from the council, after which we all clapped for two minutes, a tribute to doctors, nurses, police and bin men, working through all of this for the community, every single day.

We kept this up for three months. From a group gesture, this simple tribute quietly evolved into something deeper: a bonding of the whole community, united in hope and gratitude, a recognition of the uncertainty of the future and the unfamiliar, unwelcome conditions we had to endure. Living alone in our houses, we ventured out onto our balconies at eight o'clock and became one. The significance of the transition was certainly not lost on me. It was happening in the cities, also. News footage showed people on their balconies in a square, one playing guitar, another singing, others clapping and joining in. As a nation, it seemed we were doing the best we could to show a united front. No, Big Bad Wolf, you will not blow our houses down.

I continued chatting to Tinder guys, but now there was a subtle change. Without the chance of meeting anyone soon, I only chatted to those within spitting distance, as in a couple of hours drive maximum. Who knew how long this pandemic would last?

The interminable six weeks finally ended on Saturday, May 2nd. No major change as such, except that we were allowed to go out for a walk. Whereas cities and larger towns had designated times for the elderly, children etc. to go out for a walk, we had complete freedom, living in a village with less than a thousand inhabitants.

'Come on, Mum, let's make the most of it.' Amira was pulling on her Adidas leggings. 'Let's walk to the next village.'

I was standing by the fridge freezer, door open, about to sort out the surplus ice. Joy of joys!

'Not sure I can manage all the way, it must be, what, twelve kilometres there and back?'

'Oh mother, stop being a spoilsport, I'll be with you. 'Course you can.'

Two excruciating hours in, we arrived at the next village. My heart was pumping unusually fast, my breathing raspy and shallow, my legs shaky to the point where I could no longer feel them. Horror of horrors, at that roundabout, although two petrol stations, there wasn't a single bench or anything that could be construed as a seat. I needed to sit. Right there. Right then.

For heaven's sake, for the past six weeks, I'd only walked from the kitchen to the living room. And now she was dragging me on what seemed like Land's End to John O' Groats! Okay, nowhere to sit. There was no other option. I lay down on the grass and died.

No more than a couple of minutes later, two concerned cyclists stopped to ask if I needed an ambulance.

'Yes! Yes! Take me away!' I wanted to scream.

'No, no, she's fine,' I heard Amira explain. 'Just taking five. Thanks for your concern.'

The return journey took forever. I just couldn't seem to get my legs into gear. How Amira didn't just up and leave me I'll never know. Finally, almost five hours since we set out, we reached home. I made it shakily up the stairs, fell fully clothed onto the bed and slept right through until the next morning.

And how we suffered. My legs seized up, I couldn't sit up, let alone get off the bed and move. It was agony. And Amira, unprotected back and shoulders, all that time in the heat of the sun, was scarily red.

Yes, it was sunstroke. Oozing blisters, pain, swelling, immense discomfort for the next ten days. And all because I couldn't get my fat arse to the next village and back.

The shame washed over me in waves. Something had to change. It wasn't rocket science to see what needed to be done. I made an executive decision. The following day I felt a lot better. Alone, I walked to the one-kilometre sign and back. Two kilometres. Yay! The next day to the two-kilometre sign. And back.

My plan was to walk during the week and have weekends off, building up my stamina to see what I could achieve. By the end of two weeks, I was walking to the village: a twelve-kilometre round trip. It was taking me two hours and fifteen minutes, so I got up early to avoid the sun. I got into the habit of chatting to José, Ibiza man, most days, which was an added incentive to set out.

My legs became stronger, I lost weight — around thirteen kilos — and my body shape changed for the better. Just from walking. Who would have believed it? Suddenly I had a new-found confidence, which affected my activity on Tinder.

Cooped up for all those weeks, like a prisoner but without the guards and other inmates, I had reached out to a lot of guys, who occupied my thoughts all through the day. I now found, just by being in the open air, the blue sky and the trees, I was less interested, less dependent even, on these conversations.

I would cut it right down, I decided. Downsizing Tinder! After all, I should at some point decide who is and who isn't worth the effort. I had most of them on WhatsApp, anyway. So what I could do was hide my account for a while. Come off temporarily, with the option of restoring it if I changed my mind at a later date.

In bed that night, I battled with the app, in my quest to obscure my profile. Just as I found the right place to click, a message popped up.

Hmm, should I ignore it and get on with it anyway?

Curiosity won the day. I clicked on the message. From a Raphael. A charming message. As a first message, it knocked spots off the *"Buenos días, k tal"* I was so used to. Worth investigating a tad further. I replied. Half an hour later, he suggested WhatsApp. I agreed, wanting to get myself off Tinder yet still talk to him. We also exchanged email addresses. Already I had this little feeling in the bottom of my stomach, a flutter of something. We agreed to continue chatting in the future. I came off Tinder temporarily and looked forward to sifting the wheat from the chaff during the following days.

**

Amira had not been idle during lockdown. She had been applying for jobs and eventually secured work in the UK; a month on, a month off, leaving as soon as flights were reenabled. She managed to get one for June 15th, now just ten days away. We were both suffering from mother-daughter overload, so in a way I suppose we both imagined it would be good for us both to have a break.

Two days before she left, José told me he was travelling to stay with his sisters in Asturias, in the north of Spain, until the pandemic died down.

'There's little point in me living in a motor home if I can't travel,' he explained in his undeniably logical fashion.

Who could argue with that?

Well, hell's bells, I sure could! He was supposed to be coming to see ME. We were going to spend two weeks together, get to know each other, meet face to face for the first time, see if the spark was real. No, no, no — Asturias was the last place on earth I wanted him to go. And for how long? We had now been in contact for eight months; months filled with laughter but always with the promise of meeting up for sure by the summer. Which was now.

What about me? What about us? I wanted to protest, stamp my foot, convince him to come here first.

But at the same time, I knew there was no point. If he felt that way, then he was right to go to his sister's. He obviously didn't feel the urgency I did to set eyes on my face. Gutted didn't even cover it.

'I suppose that makes sense. At least you'll have company and a proper bed to sleep in,' was my only reply.

The following week, I left the job of downsizing my frogs; instead, trying to manage my emotions, coping with the thought of not seeing José for weeks or even months. It had been the one sure thing that had arisen out of Tinder.

And Covid had taken it away. For now.

'Get a grip,' I told myself about seventy-eight times a day.

What sweetened this bitter pill was, in fact, the correspondence with Rafa. He sent a long email, lovely messages and called once a day. I was unable to deal with anyone else. So for those few days, it was a case of sucking it up with José and hitting it off with Rafa.

And then the day arrived: 15th June, I mean. We drove to Gibraltar airport and I was astounded to be the only car in the car park, apart from two vans. The airport was like a film set before shooting: just a few people standing around. Deserted. All too quickly she had to go through security and was gone. I drove home, none of the usual delays getting out of Gib into Spain. To an empty house. No daughter. No one. Did I feel like watching a TV series? Cooking dinner? I just felt sick.

Sick and tired of it all. The realisation hit me like a slap across the face. We may have argued, but we had each other, to walk with, to eat with, to chat with, just to be with.

And now she was gone.

CHAPTER 11
A Little of What You Fancy.

Today's Specials: take a shower. Wear a nappy. Ride a horse.

My daily routine now included the morning news Channel 24 to monitor the state of affairs, daily statistics, progress and the differences between the provinces. Plus, the commentary from Dr Fernando Simón, head of medical crises. At first, he failed to warn us sufficiently, rather trying to reassure us that it wouldn't get much worse. He quickly became a familiar, household face, one we wanted to believe in, to hang on his every word. After all, he was the expert. So what went wrong?

The irony is, Spain thought it was far enough away. 'Spain will only have a handful of cases,' said Dr Simón on February 9th. Six weeks later, he reeled off daily figures of hundreds of deaths. The number of dead per capita was already three times that of Iran, and forty times higher than China. For a country 'far enough away', Spain had become the hotspot of the pandemic.

This irresponsible attitude resulted in the government reacting late and unprepared, with insufficient protective clothing for medical staff and coronavirus tests. Hospitals and care homes alike were soon overwhelmed with the increasing number of positive cases and deaths. When the army was sent into care homes, they found some residents dead in their beds. The double whammy was that, of all countries, it was China who saved the day and sent an abundance of equipment and tests.

It wasn't until May 17th that the daily death toll announced by the Spanish government fell below one hundred for the first time. June 1st was the first day without deaths by coronavirus. Finally, on June 21st, the state of emergency was lifted.

I had had just about enough. Chatting to a guy online, Carlos, who lived by the sea, I imagined myself in a flat on the coast somewhere, living simply, yet free to walk out to the sea along the beach. Free as a bird. I wanted a piece of that. And I wasn't about to hang around for it.

That very day I advertised my house for rent. I used my Tinder contacts, asking them for advice, areas to avoid etc., browsed the net and spent a few days travelling around viewing flats. I eventually secured a long-term let from September, a mere five-minute walk from the beach.

It'll be great for Tinder, I thought. A whole new set of contenders.

It was strange that, pre-Covid, I hadn't really had much experience of the dark side of Tinder. Specifically, the Perverts and Fraudsters. These days, the pervs seemed to be popping up everywhere. I suppose home alone during lockdown, time on their hands, they became more forward and suggestive online. I mean, what can the recipient do? She has a choice: go along with it or not. But for the likes of me, by this time trying to take Tinder seriously, looking for a real relationship, it's really off-putting and horrid. Having said that, it does keep you on your toes from the outset, so you are ready for any pervy onslaught. Even so, yuk!

Take Arturo from Granada. He seemed a lovely guy. For forty-eight hours. On day three, he sent me a video. I sat on the edge of my chair in shock. Stark-bollock naked, he stepped into the bath, positioned his mobile and videoed himself having a shower. Water cascading over his face, he massaged shampoo into his hair, eyes closed while he took a sponge and slowly washed himself, sweeping the soapy bubbles from one side of his chest to the other. When he reached between his legs, he began to masturbate, moaning slightly, all this facing directly into the camera. His willy sprang to attention and at that point, I turned him off.

'Lovely,' I thought. 'Not sure I fancy toad in the hole for tea tonight any more.'

The irony lingered in the air like a bad joke. He must have thought this would turn me on and I had turned him off! How was I feeling at that precise moment? Well, let's just say, had I been at the auditions for 'Psycho', I would have nailed the role of Norman Bates.

After the initial shock, I watched it again, from start to finish. And started giggling.

Oh, my days! The art of seduction personified. Not! Definitely one to share with Laura, a bestie. I didn't reply, yet he sent several text messages over the following few days and two more shower videos, as if I hadn't had my fill the first time around.

'Very generous of you, Arturo. I think I'll take a rain check. Of the forever kind,' I muttered under my breath as I blocked him.

Then there was the guy who sent me a photo of his girlfriend's vagina and asked if I was up for a threesome. I studied the photo for ages at a loss to know what it was until he asked about the *menage à trois* with him and his girlfriend. I turned it upside down and then realised what I was looking at.

What was the world coming to? For some strange reason, a quote from Eeyore, in Winnie the Pooh, sprang to mind.

"Could be worse. Not sure how, but it could be."

Come on girl, move on. Think of a more positive quote.

Owl: "If the string breaks, then we try another piece of string."

Scrolling through the contenders, I came across a certain Juan Carlos. He caught my attention from his profile blurb and was the first and only guy I right-swiped without a profile picture. I somehow wanted to chat more to this guy and then we would see what he looked like. I know — against my self-inflicted rules and also my better judgement, yet he intrigued me from the first sentence and I was tempted to explore a little further.

We chatted over the space of a few days and I agreed to go on WhatsApp in order for him to send photos and enable video calls. I was pleasantly surprised. A rugged, semi-serious expression, looking directly into the camera. Not a pretty boy but a face of character. Those first few days we really hit it off. And then he dropped the bombshell. Nappies. Yes — as in diapers. He was into nappies. At first, I assumed I had misunderstood the Spanish.

There must be another meaning for the word, I thought. I'm pretty sure he just said he was into nappies.

But I didn't need to go to the trouble of looking it up. He went on to reveal that he also liked dummies or pacifiers. He wanted to meet several times a week in my home, where I would undress him, put a nappy on him, give him a dummy and let him be a baby for a few hours. His present arrangement was costing him far too much, he explained. He had financial responsibilities, and should his wife ever found out, he'd be ruined.

Whoa! The guy's married? Hmm.

Who was I to judge? This guy had just come out and admitted he was an adult baby. Pretty foolish, when he knew by now, I was looking for a serious relationship. Why would he just come out with it like that? Was he honestly expecting me to go along with it?

I declined, politely, suggesting that Tinder probably wasn't the best place for him to resolve his issues.

'Shame,' I muttered, as I unmatched him. On paper, he was so enticing.

Having said that, I would find it hard going out with a guy called Juan Carlos. I mean they always shorten it. To 'Juanca'. The 'J' in Spanish is pronounced like an 'H'.

Say it. Out loud. Yeah, you got it.

Toni was another strange one. He lived fairly close and was anxious to meet up. Great. He had a great work ethic; an engineer, working hard all week, chatting in the evenings. We had a couple of video calls and he looked in great shape. The gym and working out were high on his leisure agenda. It all started well.

And then came the weekend. He texted.

- Hey, what are you wearing?
- A summer dress. Why?
- Free to video chat?
- Sure.

And there he was, on the sofa in all his glory, wearing nothing but a T-shirt, legs wide apart, with the longest, thickest cock I had ever seen standing to attention.

- You like?

Crikey. Oh crikey. Somehow, I managed to click off the video feature, if nothing else to breathe out! From a distance, his voice floated into my consciousness.

- You think you can handle that? I'll send you a video and you can have me every day of the week, baby. Now, your turn.

My turn? I snapped back down to earth to the familiar tone of an incoming WhatsApp message. Yes, the afore-mentioned video. Dear me. Toni was duly blocked and unmatched.

What was happening all of a sudden? Arturo, Juan Carlos and Toni in the same week? Was I changing? Choosing dodgy characters? Or was it Tinder and more people were using the app during Covid?

It was Saturday night. I needed to get out. I texted my friend.

- Laura, you free tonight? Fancy a girly night? I'll bring the wine.
- Sure, come over, bed's made up.

It was great to unwind, spend time with a bestie and actually tell someone else about all these experiences. Laura was fascinated.

'I don't know how you keep track of them all, I really don't,' she said.

'Well, this week I have a few videos,' I said, making the quote sign with my hands to the word videos. 'Fancy a cheeky peek before I delete the hell out of them?'

Today, months later, we still chuckle over that night. In the comfort of Laura's living room, we named them Shower Man, Wanker and Horse Man. It sort of became a private joke. Now not so private.

***

Sober, in the cold light of day, I think Covid was a game-changer for online dating. There was a subtle change, a change of chip; people, in general, reliant on the internet, working remotely. For Tinder, it raised the general profile to be accepted as a positive tool to find a soulmate. Before Covid, the general perception was negative, that it was full of men wanting sex, perverts, no genuine people looking for love. I decided to Google it and see if there had been a paradigm shift.

I mean quarantine, lockdown and social distancing have all taken their toll. A lot of us are struggling on without jobs, so many small businesses have folded; teachers are battling with the daunting task of online teaching, some having to juggle that with childcare at the same time. The computer screen has never featured so strongly in our lives.

Tinder experienced a surge in activity, as single people without the chance of meeting someone face to face turned to dating apps. Video calls are more popular than ever before and obviously here to stay. It's better to see potential dates in the virtual flesh, so to speak, before agreeing to meet for a coffee. Saves a lot of time in the long run.

I suppose the main change is that during lockdown, people chat for longer, get to know one another so much more before the first meeting, so that when they actually meet, it means so much more. They are not scrabbling around in the dark, wondering what to say. From the off, it's closer to their comfort zone and as such reassuring. Plus, we all have much more chance to reflect, to think things through more thoroughly during lockdown. So we have a clearer idea of what we're looking for and if this date is the one worth pursuing. This is all good news for online dating.

Coronavirus created loneliness on a global scale. Tindering was just one of the ways to alleviate that.

Funny, after my experiences, now dubbed 'Pervert Week', I have not had any since. If that's my lot, then I'll take it. Better to get it all over than spread out periodically. That would give me the heebie-jeebies and put me off Tinder for good.

I didn't dwell on this blip. I had a whole new life to look forward to. And nothing was going to spoil it.

CHAPTER 12
Scheherazade

My heroine. Witty, resourceful, dignified, brave, patient and wise, she is the storyteller in the classic collection of fairy tales, One Thousand and One Arabian Nights. Her story binds the book of fairy tales together and for me is such an inspiration. Although translated from Arabic at the beginning of the eighteenth century, her character is more relevant to modern twenty-first century society than ever.

In a nutshell, the king of India and China, Shahryar, had his wife executed for infidelity while he was away at war. He then decreed that this was a sin every woman should pay for. He married several more times, each time to a virgin. On the morning after the wedding night, they were executed. He then took Scheherazade for his wife. On their wedding night, she told him a story, so fascinating that he was enthralled. She spun it out and there was not enough time to finish it. King Shahryar, anxious to hear the end of the story, postponed her fate.

The following night, she finished the story quite quickly and began another, equally absorbing. This wonderful woman managed to keep this charade up for a grand total of one thousand and one nights, when she turned to her King and husband and admitted she had run out of stories.

Traditionally, with tragic endings so common in fairy tales, the first time I read the story, I was expecting her to be executed, and the King regrets his decision and dies a sad, wretched man. So I was further inspired to discover that they did, in fact, live happily ever after. After so long, the King had grown to love her deeply. He not only spared her life but made her his Queen.

She knew what she wanted and was prepared to wait to get there. She had her USP, great stories and her trump card, to end on a cliff-hanger. Synonymous with the KISS method: Keep It Simple, Stupid. The plan was almost stupid in its simplicity, yet enough for her to rise from wench to Queen. Impressive.

Although I was chatting to quite a few guys on a regular basis, my focus shifted to the big move. I was anxious to follow Scheherazade's example: keep things simple, be patient and smart.

'Less is more,' I said, packing away box after box of personal stuff and storing them in the garage. For the next year or so, I was going to make do with a lot less 'stuff'. A fresh start, a blank page. I was going to become Scheherazade.

Ever since motoring up to Asturias and swapping his bunk in the motorhome for a comfy super-king in his own room, communication with José had virtually dried up. On a meaningful scale, that is. Every morning, without fail, upon waking he would send me a good morning message. Then there might be a song or the odd photo, but phone calls had dried up. I understood. If you have no idea when you are likely to be able to meet someone, and the future stretches into the distance without limits or promises, then maintaining an intense distance relationship online becomes less pressing and meaningful. Regrettable, but logical and useless to contest.

After a relative lull in coronavirus cases, numbers suddenly started rising in Spain, much faster than anywhere in Europe. It was towards the end of August. The second wave was well on its way and all the restrictions that went with it. I needed to get moving. And fast.

Laura came down with me, the day of the move. September 1st. She was like a breath of fresh air. Somehow it was much more enjoyable losing my way in the city looking for the estate agents, collecting the keys and on to find the village where my new home patiently waited, than if I had been alone. Just by being there, she managed to squeeze the stress out of the situation and replace it with laughter. She stayed a whole week, bless her, changing the experience into one so incredibly uplifting.

The place was a tip, but nothing could daunt us. Within a couple of days, we had Wi-Fi installed, old mops and filthy rugs discarded, my personal pictures up and bits and bobs dotted around. We then put our heads together and rearranged the layout to be functional and homely. Sorted.

I sat back contentedly on the sofa, a glass of vino in my hand and surveyed the scene. Yes, I was going to be living in a flat the size of a postage stamp for ten months. The beach a mere five hundred metres away, the promenade with bars and a couple of restaurants, beautiful coves and bays along the coast, a warm climate, the nature reserve. My God, this was my personal piece of paradise.

I imagined José driving down to see me. They call this area the 'Ibiza' of Spain. I couldn't resist sending him a couple of photos with this information. I wasn't going to give up on us.

Rafa was waxing lyrical to me, calling me most days on WhatsApp and I had got to the point where I looked forward to his calls and also thought about him several times throughout the day. He had started to get to me, I realised. The other three didn't affect me in the same way, although we had been chatting for months.

I was Scheherazade now, I reminded myself. I would be patient, wise and dignified. No falling for guys at the drop of a hat. Be discerning. At my age, this time I had to get it right.

Despite the rising Covid cases, schools reopened in September, with all students required to wear masks. At this point, borders were still open, so I could make arrangements to meet guys from the region. I was quite excited about meeting Spaniards from Andalucía. So far everyone had been super-friendly and laid back. Did this attitude extend to single guys looking for love?

I met Pedro halfway in a bar on the beachfront, a forty-minute drive for both of us. He was polite, engaging, interested and good company. We enjoyed a lazy lunch and then went on to another bar for coffee. Time flew, conversation flowed easily and I had a great time.

And there was the rub. That certain something wasn't there. Dammit. He was lovely. But not like that, whatever 'that' was. And how the devil do you explain that to the poor guy?

We agreed to keep in touch and went our separate ways. The following day, via video call, I let him down as gently as I could. His reaction took me by surprise. He was offended, critical and angry. He ranted on for quite some time and then became offensive, at which point I hung up and left a calm, apologetic voicemail.

Remember Jacky, I told myself. It has to be the real deal. Don't settle for less. Stay dignified, patient and wise.

***

'Oh wowsers! How beautiful is this?'

I had been going for a walk every day, trying to find a decent route I could adopt for my exercise routine. I tried walking along the side of the coast road, went inland where the flamingos fed and the other way to the fort on the beach. It wasn't until Amira flew in for her fortnight break that we found it. She jogs and uses apps and things to calculate routes, distance, heart-rate and God knows what else. She found a great route down a track opposite the house for a couple of kilometres, turning off into the scrubland, through the sand dunes to the sea. Then left again, along the beach and back to the promenade for a coffee watching the sun kiss the waves. Perfect. For the time Amira was with me, I set off twenty minutes before her, walking at my usual pace and she would catch me up so that we had coffee together by the beach.

By now, October, the second wave had sunk its teeth firmly into Spain. Once again, the health service couldn't cope, saturated. Their last resort was the spare beds in intensive care. It seemed that no one 'up there' in the government was thinking straight. They lifted the lockdown far too soon in fear of the economy and then dragged their heels in responding to the surge of positive cases. This was certainly no time to risk it for a biscuit.

It could not be ignored. A massive second wave was on its way all over the world. The fact is, when lockdown was lifted, everyone went back to work. There was a huge relaxation across the board, once people were allowed out. With no clear guidelines or specific control, trams and buses were crammed full of people. It was like, 'Let's have a party and invite Covid-19.'

As of 21st October, over one million Covid cases had been reported in Spain, prompting a state of emergency to be declared on 25th October 2020. A curfew, ten p.m. to six a.m. was imposed nationwide, with autonomy given to local councils to restrict movement between regions. Bars had to close early, and no groups more than four indoors or six outdoors. Night clubs remained closed. Smoking outdoors was banned unless a two-metre distance could be maintained. Face masks and social distancing obligatory at all times.

So we had to have a reason to cross into another region, or face a steep fine. Police checks were set up to enforce the new restrictions. To fly anywhere you had to provide a negative Covid test seventy-two hours prior to flying.

All too soon, Amira flew back to the UK and her work, and I was left to my own devices. I found the daily walk invigorating. As November approached, the weather held out, sunny and warm. Just walking along the beach, the waves gently lapping my feet, sinking my toes into the sand, listening to the steady rush of the sea, had a truly calming effect on me.

Despite the strange times we are living in, I can actually say I am happy, I thought. I don't need any more than this.

Of course, this was meant in the spiritual sense. In fact, I hadn't worked for months and the coffers were running dry. But there was no use whingeing on about that. So many others were in the same boat.

If I had someone to share this simple life with, then that would be the icing on the cake. But if not, then I'm okay with that, too.

Moving to the south coast had brought with it several matches from the nearest city, Almería. Alain was one such match. French, he owned a bar/restaurant and was struggling to stay afloat. We shared a couple of calls and a week of messaging before he invited me to visit him at the restaurant.

'I will be working, but I will have time to chat to you,' he assured me. 'I can only admit a maximum of eight people inside, two tables of up to four, and three outside, and to be honest, hardly anyone is going out much. How about Tuesday, around one thirty?'

***

I was fortunate to find a parking spot a few metres away from the restaurant. On entering, Alain came over immediately, gave me the elbow greeting and led me to a table by a marble pillar. Huge paintings in gilt frames, plush velvet chairs in deep burgundy, a couple of velvet Chesterfield sofas set the scene. Reading this back, it sounds ostentatious, but it actually worked.

He managed a good ten minutes with me at the table, encouraging me to have coffee and choose a tapa, made by his own fair hand. He brought the tapas board over, recommended the *croquetas* with a French twist, and left me to serve someone at the bar.

Croquetas it is then, I thought. I never usually eat them. Just mush-fried in breadcrumbs, whether fish or ham. I can never tell the difference. Even when friends have taken me to tapas bars, famous for their home-made *croquetas* that people drool over, they didn't manage to convince me. Lots of calories for very little gratification.

He was very particular, I realised, as I watched him. He was short, yet carried himself as if taller. His clothes, smart but with his own stamp; the cufflinks, the collar up, the cravat, the black patent, pointy shoes, his moustache trimmed so precisely, above a set of gleaming white teeth. All very commendable. Not sure I could match up to that.

The *croquetas*, drizzled with a spicy, red glaze, were deliciously different on a bed of rocket and fennel, and tiny cubes of goats' cheese topped with a few drops of raspberry balsamic vinegar. Presented on a wooden block, painted black, it certainly looked the part. So he was precise in the presentation of the food, as well. I now saw that his character oozed out of the bar from the minute you stepped inside.

I looked across to his seat.

'Won't you join me?'

'*Non, non, desolé,*' he apologised. 'I must work. But please, you enjoy. I will fetch your coffee.'

Just then three women walked in and sat at the only other permitted table. He set my coffee down for me and went to greet them and take their order. He took the menu board over and returned to the bar. I could hear them chatting. In English. My view was obscured by the pillar, so I turned my attention to the coffee.

A couple of minutes went by. Then, one of the women peered around the pillar and smiled at me.

'Hiya, are you English?'

I nodded, smiling.

'Well, have you any idea what this tapas board says? We haven't a clue.'

Putting on my mask, I got up, went to their table and explained what each dish was. They ordered and introduced themselves: Jane, Mia and Agata.

Jane was English and Mia and her mother, Agata, were Swedish.

Jane had brought Agata into the city for her check-up following cataract surgery. We chatted for a little while until the food arrived and I returned to my table. Alain had been in the kitchen, and therefore unaware that we had struck up a conversation.

He soon returned and we shared a pudding he insisted I try: a sort of cheesecake but with fresh strawberries, mango and raspberries. Delish. I suppose we managed a good ten minutes, during which he was entertaining and charming. Then there was some sort of kerfuffle outside on his terrace. He ran out and Jane called me over to their table.

'Do you know the owner personally?' she asked me.

I stared back at her. What should I say? Oh, the hell with it, I'll tell her.

'No, not at all. First time today. Tinder date.'

There was a sharp intake of breath. I looked across at Mia, who had her mouth open.

'Have I said something to upset you?' I asked her.

Jane patted my arm. 'No, no. It's just that he's Mia's date, too!'

Now it was my turn to be shocked.

A million thoughts were rushing around my head. How to handle this?

I turned to face Mia. 'Really? How long have you been chatting?'

She shrugged. 'A few months now. He said to visit him whenever I wanted, but with Covid, we rarely go out. I thought it was a good opportunity to pop in today and see what he actually looked like in the flesh.'

'Well, don't worry about me. This is the first time we've met, too. We have only been chatting online for a short time. And quite frankly, I've gone right off him. So I will leave now and you can consider me out of the picture.'

'I can't believe he would do this,' she said. 'The relationship has gone on for a while and he talks about what he wants to do together in the bedroom…' She tailed off.

I leaned forward, anxious to hear more. But she got up to go outside to smoke.

I held up my hands in despair. Jane leaned towards me.

'It's true. He wants her to strut around topless, in nothing but stockings and high heels.'

'Mmm, okay, got it. I'm going back to my table now. Don't want him to see us chatting, do we?'

We exchanged phone numbers and I went back to my seat to ponder it all. You never know what goes on behind closed doors. That's when I started thinking. Maybe I do want him to know. See what his reaction would be. Yes, I would confront him.

I couldn't very well just up and leave without saying goodbye, so I waited. The girls left, promising to contact me during the week.

Fifteen minutes later, he was back. I wasted no time.

'Alain, Mia tells me you have been chatting together on Tinder for several months.'

The statement/question hung awkwardly in the air. I looked him directly in the eye.

'Mia? Well, er— yes, we have been speaking. But today is the first time to see each other. And did you see her? My God! Terrible!'

I stared at him in shock. Did he actually just say that? I realised he hadn't finished.

'Her photos are lovely but as you can see, she does not look like them.'

The disrespectful, arrogant excuse for a man! Even if he thought that, these are thoughts kept to oneself and certainly not brazenly shared with all and sundry, which at that point, I surely was.

Remember, I told myself. Dignified, patient and wise.

I thanked him for the delightful tapa and dessert. He walked me to my car, thanked me for coming and said he would be in touch.

During the following week, Alain sent me videos of him and his dog; him cooking; him walking on the seafront. He had so enjoyed our meeting and could not wait to see me again. He wanted to take the dog out with me and play together. But with the new restrictions, he said, he had no choice but to close the bar at the end of October for good. He said he would be occupied for a few weeks sorting out a way forward.

I let Mia know I had received the videos. She didn't even know he had a dog! Needless to say, she stopped chatting.

Initially, I didn't reply to his video messages. I wasn't in a good place to do so. I had to wait for Scheherazade to take over.

Finally, I was ready.

-    You have a beautiful dog. I am sure you enjoy amazing walks together. Sadly, I must decline your kind offer to play together. I'm all out of stilettos.

CHAPTER 13
Ogres and Trolls

I had been Tindering for a year now. So many Frogs, a few intermittent Perverts and a couple of Potential Princes. Shame neither had reached that potential. Prince Charming, where are you hiding? The Enchanted Forest?

And what of the Fraudsters? Yes, there had been the odd one, here and there. I suppose my lack of experience and knowledge of how they work made it easier for them to hone in on me. As such, I was an easy target. Vulnerable, looking for love. So that's what they preyed on.

Take oil-rig guy, Frank. He asked me to log onto Hangouts so we could communicate more easily. I had never heard of Google Hangouts but agreed. He said as soon as he had a vacation, we could video-chat all day, but on the rig, it wasn't allowed. I saw the logic of that. With the parameters of the relationship set up, we began chatting. Not every day — sporadically, in fact. He was a widow with a son in the USA, looking for a serious relationship. It went on for a few months. He started sending pictures of flowers for me and love hearts, saying how his heart was filled with joy when we chatted. I thought a few of his messages were a bit strange, as if he could have said this to any woman. Somehow, they didn't strike me as meant only for me. Here are just a few examples:

- I'm not interested in your physical beauty, I just need the one that makes my heart glad.
- Faithfulness and sincerity is the key for building a solid relationship that will be based on trust
- And then the excuses for not sending photos:
- I don't have current photos: they are all old pictures, as you know the situation here on the Baltic high sea.

I asked him to take a photo there and then. His reply: I can't because I chat from a desktop

After these rather static-type messages, his tone suddenly changed and all he could talk about was his son who was missing him and how he wanted to send him a new mobile as a present. Could I help? Of course, he would pay me back as soon as he left the rig.

My initial reaction was one of shock, simply because I would never dream of asking for money from a guy I'd never met. As it was, I was broke; a fact he was unaware of, but even so! There were a thousand other people I would spend money on before him.

I said no, he would have to ask someone else — a relative or friend in the USA, for example. He came right back at me with inane excuses, ever more insistent, making me feel awkward. He certainly had never shown so much passion when waxing lyrical all these months. Now I was seeing the real guy for who he was. Pathetic. The more he pressed me, the more I resisted until I snapped.

- Look, douchebag, it's like this. No. Don't ask again. We're done.

It was like I hadn't spoken. He continued to message me, pleading, playing the guilt card; in fact, every card in his sorry little book until the following day when I blocked him.

It took a while, a few glasses of red and good friends on the phone to get over what had kicked off. So there it was. A Fraudster. I had been introduced to the world of scammers.

***

Crack!

What was that? What had I broken now?

Shaking out the throw on the sofa, the edge had caught my glasses on the top of the bookcase and sent them flying. They went crashing to the ground at a rate of knots. My favourite pair.

I picked them up and stared miserably at the irreparable mess in my hand.

It's a sign, I thought. These were my rose-tinted glasses, the ones I felt comfy and safe in. And I have just shattered them with a sweep of a sofa throw.

Right then. Glasses off. Open your eyes, Jacky Trevane. Wise up.

I turned my attention to Bob.

Slowly, the mist clouding my judgement so far began to clear. But there was no way I was out of the woods yet. There was a lot to learn and I was only at first base. I had changed my chip and opened the door to the possibility that some guys would say anything to gain your trust.

I reviewed what I knew about him. A widower, working on a ship, hence no video calls. Wanting to relocate at the end of his contract. Professing his love for me now, openly, talking about being a family, together with his son, even though I didn't reciprocate any of his feelings. Once again, I realised, it was as if he didn't get it. He just churned out the messages whatever my reaction. If I disagreed, he brushed over it.

I decided to test him.

- Bob, remember last week I told you about my perfect weekend? You never told me what you thought. Are we on the same page here?

His answer gave me mine.

- Baby, you are everything to me, the first thing that I think of in the morning. Tell me what you are doing now.

This is Bob
Bob tried to trick Jacky
Jacky was wise
Jacky blocked Bob
Be like Jacky.

***

The 'copy-and-paste' scammers started to crawl out of the woodwork. Some of these were the first I was able to recognise.

One guy, Nick, extremely attractive, contacted me on 15th November. After a quick *'¡Hola!'*, he launched immediately into his questions.

- I want to know more about your family, background, life experiences, past relationships, goals and dreams.

Crikey, get straight to it why don't you? A one-liner formed my response.

- Hi, English, three kids, looking forward to a bright future. You?

His reply came straight back, after a nanosecond. Another clue, as clearly, he had no time to type the following. Neither was it an answer to my question.

- Thank you for your message. Life is full of uncertainty and you must experience the two sides of every coin in the life course. The good news is that we have a wonderful God who always restores our lost Glory when we think that all hope is gone. Thank God for your life. My intention to go to the site is to look for a woman who brings me the happiness I lost years ago when I lost my wife. You're a beautiful woman, I'd love to spend the rest of my life with someone like you. But as it is, I don't know if you can decide and I'll love to be with someone like you. But we just wanted to say that God has his own way of designing a good fate. I really care about you.

Hold on a minute, he really cares about me? After what — ninety seconds?

No point wasting valuable time on this geezer. I decided to remain dignified. (Thank you, Scheherazade.)

- Okay, so let's leave it at that. I wish you every success in your quest to find your better half.

Once again, in 'Frank' mode, it was as if I hadn't written a thing. As I read the following message, it hit me. He's talking to himself. These are copy-and-paste messages. Not a single reference to me or anything I say. He's a Fraudster.

The message was more like an essay. Nothing that could be remotely linked to me personally, considering this was still Day One of our conversation, plus the fact that he was American, yet using the Spanish translator to send me messages in Spanish because he assumed I was Spanish. Hell, he hadn't even asked me my name!

- I read your message. Your friendship and love, and all the wonderful things they bring to my life are like nothing else I have ever known. My heart is complete with the love we share and our love becomes more beautiful every day. I love you and while we're together I have everything I need. You're always with me… In a smile, I remember, feeling and every moment. You will always be mine forever, love. If I knew how to write a song, I would write one every day that I would say that I am in love with you and why I feel that way. I love you a lot. I feel like I have known you for many years and I don't know why, but I feel a lot about it. I just can't get you out of my mind, I really want to be near you because I've had a lot of things going on in my head lately. I have trouble putting my thoughts into words, so you'll have to be naked with me through this. I keep thinking about the future, about life and what I want to get out of it. I keep thinking about us and what this relationship means to me. I keep thinking about these things, and I realise they're going hand in hand. This relationship is my future; it's what I want from life. I want to grow old with you. I want to experience this crazy love for centuries, and I really think I'm going to experience it. I want us to walk through new houses choosing which one is suitable for us. I want to see you walk around our house in a big T-shirt with loose hair and catch me looking at how beautiful you are. I want you to take my blankets off at night, and then I have to come even closer, if possible, to keep you warm.

This is Jacky
Jacky didn't trust Nick
Jacky was wise
Jacky blocked Nick
Be like Jacky.

***

After all those months, I wasn't faring very well with the long-distance guys, I realised. Of the original three, only Ben remained. His turn to go under the microscope.

But before I got round to it, he changed the goalposts. Drastically.

In five months, he had sent me only three photos. One in his white coat, at work, as a doctor for the UN, one at the gym and one in a garden. No video or voice calls. Again, a widower with a daughter who was living in Liverpool, he said. Every morning, without fail, he sent me little messages to start my day. Nothing like José's, who would say, 'Morning J, beautiful sunrise this morning. Enjoy your day.' Ben's messages were more or the 'May your day be blessed with the warmth of the sun, blah blah blah.' Again, totally impersonal. Yet constant.

Then a couple of weeks ago he asked me for a full body shot. I found one from summer and sent it, but he said he wanted one with me naked! I just laughed.

- When we meet, then maybe, but some things in life we have to wait for.

He protested, saying he was so lonely, he had needs, and I didn't know what he was going through.

I had given him my answer. I wasn't about to discuss it further. He wasn't a child and had to respect that.

When the penny dropped, he changed his tune and lowered the tone further, to talk about sex. He wanted a picture of my vagina, and asked me to touch myself and video it.

This was a new side of him; one he had previously kept firmly under wraps. I began to wonder how many other sides he was hiding. Doubt was setting in, for sure. I decided to nip this in the bud.

- This is never going to happen, so please, enough already. You have the wrong girl. NOT INTERESTED.

His reaction was to go dark for a few days. As it happened, these days coincided with the Bob experience. Frank was also fresh in my mind and with Ben off the radar, it gave me time to step back and see how little I knew him.

His morning missive popped up midweek. He made no reference to our earlier conversation, rather focusing on his bad mood. He said he was having trouble with his internet account and no access to funds until the end of the month. Could I help out by sending two-hundred euros? I refused immediately, offering no excuse. Surprisingly, he left it and said he didn't know when he would be in touch.

One week later he was back. Boomerang Ben. Still in a bad mood. His daughter was in financial difficulty and his money was all tied up. He needed two thousand euros from me. Today.

He didn't even wrap it up in excuses. Just gave it to me straight. Of course, I refused. And then that bastard showed his true colours.

- Well, my dear, you may think you're safe, by refusing to send me erotic photos of yourself, but believe me, you are not. Pay me the money today or you will be sorry. I have several headshots from you. I will post these of you involved in pornographic, filthy acts across the internet, to all your contacts, to your friends and family. Facebook, Instagram, Twitter, Linkedin. Everywhere. You have twenty-four hours.

OMG. What the—? It took a while to sink in.

I wanted to spit back at him, 'Do your worst, lowlife. Bring it on!'

But a little voice, my voice of caution, spoke out.

What if he could Photoshop, or whatever the hell they do? What if...

The question hung in the air, unanswered.

Be careful, Jacky, I thought. You need to play this one right.

Twenty-four hours. Shoot, that was nothing. Okay, let's deal with that first.

Shaking, I typed my reply:

- I need more time. During Covid, I haven't been earning and times are hard. I will have to negotiate a loan. Could you let me have a week to sort this out? This is my best offer.

He replied immediately.

- Okay.

117

Phew, I had bought some time. I sank down to the floor and burst into tears.

Tea. I need a cup of tea.

It's so true. A cuppa makes the world seem brighter.

There's strength in numbers, I decided. Sometimes, that's what friends are for. Warming my cheek with the cup, I methodically called three of my besties and one of the men for whom I did freelance work. Four completely different characters; each one intelligent and resourceful in their unique way.

They were unanimous in their initial reaction, however. Horrified, disgusted and sympathetic. And then they put their rational heads on and considered the problem.

My boss offered me the services of his lawyer, a man of considerable distinction in his field.

'Jacky, I mean it, he is at your service. This man cannot get away with this. Put together as much information as you can about him and send it across.'

My friends pointed out that Facebook would never accept pornographic material on the site, so in that respect I was safe.

- Which platform are you using to chat to him?
- Hangouts. Why?
- That's linked to Google. So he can access your email. Close it down and get off it. You can also erase all the conversations and delete all photos

sent permanently. So if he hasn't yet used your photo, there might be time to remove it before he does.

Of course! Why hadn't I thought of that? I hung up and went into Hangouts, deleted all the photos and conversation, blocked him and signed out.

The following day, bolstered by the support of my friends, I logged into my LinkedIn account, looking for work, trying to keep Boomerang Ben at the back of my mind. There were four friend requests. Unlike Facebook, where I vet all the requests and ignore the majority, the purpose of LinkedIn was to enlarge my network. I was therefore used to accepting all requests without a second glance.

That day, however, I noticed the second one was from a "Benjamin 101, UN doctor"! Oh my! He was hoping to slip through the net and I could so easily have accepted him. Suddenly I was a bag of nerves all over again. I refused his friend request and spent the day trawling through my internet groups, looking for him. Nothing.

Come on, what can he do? Just leave it.

A week went by. I decided it was a hollow threat; one meant to scare me. Oh boy, it had certainly worked. I hadn't slept properly, and without my friends, I would have been a nervous wreck.

So when the email appeared in my inbox, I stared at it in disbelief. What? How? And more importantly, why?

-   Ha, ha, you are so very stupid. You think by closing Hangouts I cannot reach you? Think again. I have patiently wait for you to have a rethink, now that you refused responding. I have no choice than publishing your erotic pictures and video to your family and friends.

I felt sick. He had accessed my email account. What more could he do?

I called Laura.

"Don't worry, Jacky, the email address is connected to Google, so he could have accessed that info from the moment you started chatting. He can't get into any other account."

Unconvinced, I deleted my Facebook, Twitter and Instagram accounts and created a new Gmail account. I couldn't take any more chances. Now I was scared.

Of course, I didn't reply. The following day he sent this:

-   Listen to me I am been so patients with you and you haven't had a change of mind I think I will do the needful with those pictures and videos so you have your options. All you need to do is assisting my daughter with two thousand euro.

Before deleting every link to do with him that I could think of, I copied the last two messages and kept them in a folder on my laptop. Who knew if I would need them further down the line?

And that was it. It has been three months now. I have set up new accounts, but every now and then, I look on Facebook or LinkedIn for a "Benjamin 101." He is no longer there.

I can't help wondering who he is masquerading as now, and with whom.

***

So here we were, in November, seeing Andalucía in its own bubble, like many other municipalities. Now all non-essential activities had to close, including non-essential shops. Bars and restaurants were only open until six pm. Curfew hours increased from ten pm until seven am. Andalucía, as a whole, closed its borders to travellers from the rest of Spain. A couple of weeks later, you had to produce a negative Covid test in order to fly, and then self-isolate on arrival.

It became clear to me that meeting guys was off the agenda for the foreseeable future. So I turned my attention to Rafa, my one remaining saving grace. My

PPC, Potential Prince Charming. Boy. Was I ready for him!

Where to start? Well, after the first few days of messaging and calling, we exchanged emails. His first letter impressed me. He had told me some of his background, but to take the time to write it down was a plus in my book.

This is what he wrote:

- I hope by the time you get to read my message it makes you smile. Well, I just wanted you to know that it has been a great pleasure getting to knowing you, and I always enjoy hearing that cute lovely voice of yours... Honestly, I must say it was also very inspiring seeing your profile the first time I contacted you and I must commend you had a lovely profile picture. I am out here looking for a serious relationship as vehemently opposed to jumping in the sack only. Looking forward to knowing more about you as anticipated by me and also sharing all about me with you. Well, maybe I should start by telling you a little about myself. I was happily married for 23 years until my wife died 8 years ago. I always thought we would eventually be one of those older retired couples you see walking at the mall hand in hand or sitting on a park bench. So, I never dreamed I would be dating again in my life. I am a businessman who deals on furniture and interior designs. I do really love my job, though sometimes complicated but it is always a fun-sight. I find it very interesting because it is also one of the few things that I love to get lost into as it exposes me traveling at intervals around various continents. I do not necessarily consider distance a barrier to finding true love and affection. When familiarity and affection grows, the distance fades rapidly away, having an unreserved respect for fellow humans and especially the little ones is a must and a plus to my person. I was raised a Christian but really have a strong spiritual belief in the spirit within us all so it is not tied to formal religion but encompasses a wonderful openness to the energy around us and the beauty in the world. My family is a very small one I must say. Me and my son, (My father passed on when I was only 7 years of age). So I was raised by a foster father who was more like a husband to my mother and a father to me, but he also passed on in 2013. So now I only have my mother left back in Canada and she is very old now. I love kids a lot and spend a better part of my free time with him (my son) I have a Westphalia Volkswagen van that I love to go camping in with. I also have a motor that keeps me on the water as well, other than chartering sailboats. I love adventure but love to come home to a cosy home where I keep all my treasures. A free-spirited Nester!

There were others, equally eloquent, combined with calls. It was a bit awkward because of the time difference, but he still made the effort. After the first couple of months, the calls were on a daily basis. He was in Maryland, USA, but planning to bring his business to Spain and eventually retire on the Costa del Sol. Had it not been for Covid, he would already be there, he explained. He had an agent looking for potential places.

He wooed me. I lapped it up. An incurable romantic, for my sins, we were soon in romantic mode. He put a smile on my face when there was no real reason to smile.

In July, he secured a contract in Dublin. Despite the restrictions, the company flew him and six employees out in a private jet. It was a two-phase, six-month project, with a six-week break in between.

We both agreed we should spend those six weeks together and see exactly where our relationship was going.

Everything changed for the better once he was in Ireland. There was only an hour's time difference; plus, he was in Europe and had managed to cross the ocean. And the job was going so well. He was happy. We were happy. When he told me I had turned his world upside down, I felt the same.

He spoke to Laura, and also my granddaughter when she visited in August. He was always interested in my family and making plans for us in the future.

On September 8th, his agent booked him a ticket to fly over to me. I was super excited. I did a special shop, cooked a mushroom risotto from scratch and lemon chicken goujons. He sent me the details. But then, one of their machines failed. It was a major setback, bringing the last week of Phase One to an abrupt halt. The wind changed. Rafa became anxious, failing to secure a new machine, at a cost of (he said) sixty thousand euros. He eventually found one and asked me if I would do the transfer from my laptop. He didn't want to make such a large purchase from a company's public computer, having been hacked in the past. So, I sat in front of my computer, he supplied his bank details and I wired his money to pay for the machine. The whole process took five minutes.

'Sorry, love. I will have to oversee the delivery and the revised deadline. Don't worry, I will be with you before you know it,' he reassured me.

A few days later, he asked me to wire more money from his account to cover materials. Nineteen thousand euros this time. The machine arrived, and he had forgotten about the tax. It was not much money, but he asked me to do a transfer for it. Each time, I sent him a screenshot of the transaction. But this time was different. A message appeared on the screen:

- Due to the suspicious origin of this transaction, your account is restricted. Please call into the office to resolve the matter.

On hearing this, Rafa went into overdrive. What could he do now? He couldn't exactly fly back to the States and casually stroll into the bank. They refused to lift the restrictions over the phone or online. How was he going to pay his workers? They were all due to be paid at the end of this Phase. Now what?

I was distraught. I had never heard him so upset, sounding so desperate.

When he called me that evening, he confessed that he had worked hard his whole life and reaped the rewards; that he had never experienced problems like this before, and he didn't have a clue where to start. I suggested he try his secretary, Tracey, but beyond that, was as useless as a chocolate fireguard.

Phase One was finally finished and signed off, and he sent me confirmation of another flight: this time, 20th September.

- I need to get to you. The transactions were made on your laptop, and I need to be in the same place so they send the papers over to your address to lift the restrictions on my account. It should take a couple of weeks. Thank God my workers are so understanding.

On September 18th, he said he'd received a letter from the Irish government and was being detained! He even sent me a pdf of the letter. It had his name, the company, address, every detail on it, with the government letterhead, saying that unless he paid the outstanding tax bill for his contract, he would not be allowed to leave Ireland.

He had not been made aware of the fact that because he was neither an Irish national nor resident, he had to pay a surtax on the contract, as a foreign contractor. This was a percentage of the price of the job, nearly two million euros. So quite a hefty amount. They took his passport and let him return to his lodgings, but said he had to sign in every day until the bill was paid.

Once again, he missed his flight. His spirits dropped, he was constantly on the phone to his secretary and others to secure a loan here, a loan there. September gave way to October and then November.

My friends were telling me he was fake, to give him up. Their words made perfect sense. We had never had a video call. Why the hell not, they demanded to know. Get him to sort his phone out, borrow someone else's, go to an internet café, download Skype... It's true: there were endless ways of video calling but he blamed it on his old phone and I went along with it. Amira was disgusted, even grabbing the phone and telling him, in no uncertain terms, never to speak to her mother again and that he made her sick.

I was still hanging on to our vision for a life together. He was perfect for me, and I wasn't about to give up when the going got rough.

By November, he had amassed quite a bit of his debt from business friends and a couple of loans. He could finally see light at the end of the tunnel and began to talk again about coming home to me. However, nobody could travel without a negative Covid test, and an 'essential reason.' We weren't sure that sorting his bank problems fitted the brief.

He was two thousand, two hundred and fifty euros short. On December 3rd, he asked me to help. He knew my financial position exactly and that I was not in a position to help, even if I could. When I repeated this back to him, asking why he would even ask, he said it would prove I loved and trusted him. He told me how others had found money for him and he hoped I would find a way — take out a loan, ask a friend — to get the last bit.

My Prince Charming would never have done that to me. The fog was clearing. My fairy tale, living happily ever after with this wonderful man, was exactly that. A fairy tale. Not real. Merely stuff that dreams are made of.

I just couldn't believe it. I felt numb. In bed that night, when he called, I was tempted to ignore it, but curiosity got the better of me. Shakily, I picked up the phone.

It was noisy, like a busy café, children shouting and playing, men all chatting, talking over one another.

'Rafa? Rafa?' I yelled.

Nothing. He had obviously called me in error. I was about to click it off when it occurred to me that the voices were not English. Quickly, I pressed loudspeaker and strained to make out any bits I could.

Well, it certainly wasn't any European language; nor Arabic, nor any Eastern language like Mandarin. Not Russian either, but wait — yes, it could have been an African language, like Swahili. Yes, I decided, it most definitely was.

A man suddenly raised his voice, supposedly at a child, shouting 'Javi!' and then chastising him. I listened for close to three minutes. This was a busy café, either in an African community in Ireland or… I didn't want to go there, but by now it was becoming crystal clear. A café somewhere in Africa.

***

He called me the following morning. I burst into tears and told him about the call. He said he hadn't called me yesterday and he had no idea what I was talking about. He had no explanation other than a bad connection.

I told him I no longer believed him and that he had shattered my dream. That he had played the long game, but at the end of the day, for what — two thousand euros? Six months, tricking someone, who doesn't have the money, anyway? That he wasn't the smart guy he had made himself out to be.

He continued to insist he was that guy, that one day he would come knocking on my door, with a smile and open arms, and I would see how wrong I had been about him. He hung up, saying he loved me.

That was the last message I ever had from Raphael Wallin Wiklund.

CHAPTER 14
The Pied Piper with Red Flags

Shell-shocked after Rafa's deception, I went into the classic first stage of grief: that of denial. He knew my address. He would come knocking in the next few days. I developed a relationship with my pillow, burying my face in its comfort, imagining me opening the door to find him smiling on the doorstep. It wasn't as if I could confide in anyone. My friends — hats off — had been stalwarts, supporting me throughout his excuses, week after week after week, until gradually they twigged that there were more than a few red flags flapping in the breeze. One by one, they withdrew, leaving me and my pillow, willing him to be real.

Yes, I know. I was blind. Blinded by hollow words and promises. It took me two whole weeks to share any of it, and then only with family and close friends. It was weird. Emotionally, I felt as if I had been violated, yet at the same time I had invited all of it. Rafa had got right under my skin. How to reconcile that?

'You bastard!'

Yes. I got angry. The slimy, deceitful, immoral little scumbag. I was beginning to process what had been happening and frankly, I hated all of it. My anger, directed at him primarily, didn't last. Like thunder, it began to rumble and build up until it came crashing down. On me. How could I have been so damned stupid? What was I thinking? Why didn't I listen to my friends and family? For pity's sake, Amira was never convinced from the first moment. I thought back to the time she had grabbed the phone and told him in no uncertain terms that if he didn't stop speaking to 'my mother', she would report him; that he was a twenty-something scammer and he'd better watch out! I had been mortified, full of remorse. He had just laughed gently and told me not to worry: it was completely natural for children to worry about their parents when online dating. Especially as there were so many scammers around. That when he came to live with me, she would see how wrong she was. I had lapped up every word. Jeez!

If only I had listened to them, things would never have got so out of hand.

Two weeks in, I forgave myself. It wasn't a gradual process. I woke up, saw the morning sun streaming through the window, and there and then made a mental note that today was the first day of the rest of my life. No more berating myself. No more self-indulgence, feeling sorry for myself and definitely no more anger.

'I forgive me,' I said to my reflection while cleaning my teeth. 'Get over yourself. Move on.'

Of course it wasn't so simple. But simply recognising the negative treadmill I had climbed onto and deciding to jump off was a great start. Plus, the shift in attitude helped me appreciate the beautiful day and count my blessings. I didn't introduce the subject, yet I didn't run away from it either when friends brought it up. I manned up and told them straight that I had been scammed.

A rollercoaster. The perfect word to describe both my feelings and learning curve on this intrepid journey. Leaving me pretty battered and bruised.

***

We all know that time is a great healer. Bruises and memories alike gradually fade. So before things got to that point with me, I wanted to be sure I took something positive away from the whole experience. Specifically, to be acutely aware of everything I had learned in order to be ready for the next scumbag. To learn and grow stronger.

Not only that but to be able to get it out there and spread the word for other desperate, vulnerable yet naive people; an easy squeeze for these amoral reprobates. As a heads-up:

"To secure ourselves against defeat lies in our own hands, but the opportunity of defeating the enemy is provided by the enemy himself."
— Sun Tzu

The more we know about our enemy, the more we can identify his weaknesses. Information is power. And I had gathered a fair amount on my personal Tinder rollercoaster.

Adopting the role of The Pied Piper, I want to reel in as many of these dirty Rats as possible. Instead of a pipe, I will carry flags. Red flags.

Rat Trap List:

16 scarlet-red flags

• Professions: doctors for the UN, drilling engineers, IT technicians, always based abroad or offshore on contracts. *This gives them an out for normal WiFi coverage, an excuse for internet problems.*

• They usually mention their salary, to be received at the end of the contract, which is often in the millions. *This is to make you feel secure financially and bond with them more quickly.*

• They are hoping to retire and locate to wherever you are. *Again, a ploy to make you feel secure; that you will not be asked to uproot your current life and relocate for them.*

• They say they are widowers, with one or two kids, more often than not just the one. Wife dying in childbirth is a common one. Fatal car accident crops up a lot too. *This is playing the sympathy card.*

• They don't send many photos and are "not allowed" to make video calls. Or their phone is on the blink. *Well, if you saw what they actually looked like…*

- On the first day they show real interest in how long you have been on the site and if you have had any bad experiences. They are super interested in this. If you say yes, then they will press for more details and how you handled it and if you gave any of them money. If you say you have been scammed, they will say they have, too. *This is for you to feel you have something in common as victims and look for something more genuine. Also, for them to get intel on your attitude and experience of scammers.*

- They send a message every morning, but in the form of a quote — never personal — one that could be sent to multiple women. *These are the copy and paste merchants. One size fits all. The 'uni-message.' To make you believe you are the first person they think about upon waking.* (Don't yawn — it works! It's what they depend on.)

- Their messages are often general, stating what they value in a relationship, or what kind of guy they are. *Again, this is from a bank of messages they select from, copy and paste.*

- Their English is what you might call a bit 'off' at times. For example, Rafa said, 'I'm just going to brush my tooth,' among other little things. *Don't be fooled into seeing this affectionately as a quirk. It really is a red flag. If you tune in to this, it could be their Achilles heel.*

- They ask a lot of questions but rarely answer all of yours. *This is to amass as much info about you as possible, early on. All they have to do is copy and paste one of their responses about them. In this way they can handle several 'victims' at once.*

• They will flatter you day after day, repeating the same things. Your hair, eyes or voice. *This is to test your reaction and see how you respond to flattery, to suss out your character. If you respond favourably, then it makes their job a shedload easier.*

• They say they are new to the dating site, that their son/daughter pressed them to start looking for a new woman to love. If you ask, they will usually say a couple who didn't work out. *This is to make you think they are not talking to any other women.*

• After a week or so they will start talking about love, how you are the one for them and only you. They want to build a life with you. *Here, they are planting the seed of a long-term relationship, which leads to trust.*

• Further down the line, when they deem you to be primed and ready, they will hit you with the moody card. Suddenly they are anxious, stressed. They might go a day without contacting you. *This is to get you to press them for details, to show your support and that you care.* If you don't, they know they have to work on you a little longer and snap out of their mood. If you try to help, they know they are in. Game on!

• They often drag this out. You press for details. They are reluctant, unwilling to put their problems on your shoulders. They are waiting for you to reassure them that you really do want to help, whatever the problem. *This is their trump card. This is to make you feel that you have the power to help and therefore you really should help the guy out, whatever the problem.*

• Finally, those who ask for money for their phone, not a huge amount, are merely testing the waters before the big ask. *This is a red flag for bigger things to come.* Say no.

The thing is, Frank, Ben and Rafa all utilised quite a few of those red flags yet, until Rafa, I didn't learn a damn thing. Like Sun Tzu points out, now I am aware of a few red flags, I am in a stronger position to recognise and oust a scammer. The more we learn about their tactics, the sooner we can kick them to the kerb.

***

Sometimes I let my guard down and my thoughts wander back over the six months I had with Rafa: the Rafa who does not exist; the Rafa who thankfully didn't manage to sting me for thousands. And maybe it's precisely because of that that I am not bitter about any of it. I was truly happy, for a period of months, despite lockdown, economic instability and an unrecognisable, crazy world.

And the reason for my happiness was Rafa. I just can't bring myself to be sad about that. Bastard!

CHAPTER 15
Hindsight is a wonderful thing

The more I spoke to victims of online-dating scammers, the more I realised that there were some real pros out there, going for the long game, drawing you in, pulling at your heartstrings, using any information to seduce and convince you. Throw the wonders of technology into the mix and they come close to invincibility. The only variable not in their favour is in their choice of victim.

Take Rafa, for example. He didn't know anything of my past; if I was weak, strong, rich or poor. And he never ever asked. He chose to present himself as the perfect, romantic gentleman. Such a guy would never mention finances. Fortunately for me, he didn't have the means to fake video calls, instead convincing me he was a traditional man with little techno knowledge and would sort his phone out when he had time. In eight months, he never found that time.

Not so, however, with Marion. German, in her early fifties, she is fit, intelligent and extremely attractive. She began chatting with a guy from the US military. His photos were, frankly, gorgeous, and he provided quite a few in different locations. One in the car driving, another lying on his bed, another in uniform. He said he was due to retire in December 2020 and would relocate to Germany to be with her. He was sweet, complimentary, attentive and seemed genuine. Marion loved the way he spoke to her and responded in kind, until they were locked in what she thought was a 'proper' relationship, telling each other everything about themselves. She would wait excitedly for his calls, respond to his every message. She was falling in love.

The first bombshell came when he informed her that he was being sent to Afghanistan and so would be delayed. He backed the story up with photos, and she never gave it a second thought. She trusted him completely.

Then he informed her that he had saved the lives of some rich people in Afghanistan, who had rewarded him with gold bars to the value of around one hundred thousand dollars. Could he send them to her to keep until he arrived?

'Of course, my darling. No problem,' was her immediate reply.

She provided both her home and email addresses and he went to Kabul to send the package. Three days later, she received an email to say the delivery had been shipped. Days after that, the company Mercury Express emailed her to say the package had reached Istanbul, but to leave the country there was an outstanding tax of five thousand dollars to be paid. The company provided a tracking number and they had a support centre on their website, all which worked when she checked it out. So, at this point, she had no reason to believe anything was amiss.

Shocked, she contacted Mr Wonderful, who merely sent her details of a bank account to pay the money into. Not having the full five grand, she told him she could only raise two thousand dollars at that moment, so what should they do?

- That's fine, my love. Transfer the two thousand. If I manage to get back to the USA within the next three weeks, I can pay the remainder, no problem. I have just been told I have just two weeks to go here in Afghanistan. Otherwise, try to get the three thousand for me in the next three weeks. Don't worry, my love. We will be together soon, with all the money we need.

So Marion dutifully went ahead with the transfer of two thousand dollars. And although she received multiple emails from the courier company, the gold bars never arrived.

A niggle, that's all it was. At the back of her mind. One which, in the end, made her go onto the Facebook site, 'Scammers United'. And guess what? There was his picture, as large as life!

It took a while to sink in. But there he was in all his glory. Only it wasn't him. Just some poor guy whose photo had been commandeered to prey on innocent victims.

When reality finally dawned, Marion contacted her bank, and the police, but he had covered his tracks well. The bank to which she thought she was sending the money didn't exist; it was a number resembling a bank account but in fact was some sort of card, used just to receive money, and untraceable. The transport company had to be fake as well. This had been a grand setup, one which any vulnerable person would fall for.

Now a little stronger, she messaged him to say she knew. After all that, the bastard eventually caved in told her he was from Nigeria and he was sorry!

Hello?

Naturally, she blocked him.

Marion is an engineer and to all intents and purposes has a beautiful life and just wants to find a good man to love and build a life with him. No more, no less. She, like me, can't believe how she was so devoted to a guy she had never met, and then blindly send him money. Hindsight is a wonderful thing.

This experience can happen to anyone. Whatever your character, whether you are intelligent, cautious, flighty or spontaneous, as long as you have an ounce of vulnerability and hope that you can find love, you fit the brief. Which more or less covers most of the single global market. The bad boys and girls out there are all over it. And getting better at it.

**

Researching for this book, I came across an extreme example of scammers at work that beggars belief, widely published online in 2019. In fact, it was the bank that gave rise to suspicion, alerting the police when an eighty-year-old woman from Singapore withdrew eight hundred thousand dollars in cash without giving a reason, and then scheduled further withdrawals. It transpired that she had fallen for someone posing as a Chinese government official. She fervently refused to be convinced he was a scammer, rejecting all attempts made by the police to help. She was known to be a smart lady, believing she would recognise a scam when she saw it. The police continued with their investigations and managed to secure the arrest of three runners (the guys used to collect the money) involved in the scam. But this took time, and she had been sanctioning withdrawals all the while. At the time of the arrests, she had lost more than $3.6 million.

Yes, it beggars belief. But that's the point. We are all vulnerable at some point and too damned stubborn to believe it is happening to us. You must recognise that old chestnut: scams happen to other people, 'cos I am smarter than that. Sadly, famous last words for thousands of us. My scam with Rafa was only different in the respect of the money. His tactics mirrored the ones in play with the lady above. You win some, you lose some and you move on.

Another poor guy, in his seventies, lost his life savings to his online sweetheart, who convinced him she needed breast cancer surgery, and to pay off her debts, so she could leave her job to be with him.

And there's the rub. Emotional blackmail. Preying on the emotionally needy. This man, a conservative, formerly frugal guy was writing cheques for up to one hundred thousand dollars at a time, unaware that his 'princess' was buying a new house, extra land, new equipment for the family farm and so on. This story has the added element of tragedy, because he suffered from Alzheimer's and was unaware that he was a victim for the whole duration. Or maybe that's a blessing. In this particular case, the authorities pounced on it and repossessed much of the assets the scammer purchased and were able to return a decent percentage of the monies lost to spend on his medical care.

**

I reached out to a few of the members on Facebook claiming to have been scammed, to hear their stories. One, Bella, said she had been scammed not once, but twice. I sent her a private message to hear her story. She asked me quite a few questions at first. I told her a little of my situation, to help her trust me. She eventually said she would put something together and get back to me the following day. The next day she sent me a friend request. I ignored it. Then she messaged me:

- Hi, can I trust you with something?
- Of course.
- My late Dad lawyer wanna send me a check to clear my bill so I want you to help me cash it out for me cause I don't have a bank account so I can clear my bills. Please can you help me?
- Wow. You really take the biscuit.
- I don't understand.
- The hell you don't!
- Are you helping me or not?
- Take a wild guess.
- I don't like guessing.
- I am now reporting you.
- It was just a prank. I thought I have a new friend but no.

I shook my head in disbelief. The absolute gall of these people. They will try anything. Good job I hadn't accepted her as a Fb friend.

This is Bella
Bella is sly and tried to trick Jacky
Jacky saw through Bella
Jacky blocked Bella
Be like Jacky.

The more stories I heard, the more I realised this was not a case of a few isolated cases. It was everywhere I looked. Chatting to one of my friends, Jess, the conversation turned to Rafa and she told me about her aunt in Dorset. In her seventies, widowed for two years, she set up a profile on Tinder. Her profile picture showed her standing outside her chocolate-box cottage on a summer's day. She was soon chatting to a guy in Canada, who got under her skin fairly quickly with his compliments and persistence. Once again, he told her Facetime wasn't possible, which she accepted, at that stage needing to believe him.

'Within a matter of weeks, she was besotted,' Jess explained. 'It got ridiculous. I went down to visit her for the weekend and she was acting like a smitten teenager. She kept his photo in a frame by her bed, which she kissed goodnight. It was obvious to me straight away. I mean, he was gorgeous, at least twenty years her junior, and had told her he was in love after a week!'

'So what did you do?' I asked.

'The same as her friends. Tried to talk some sense into her. I mean, with her daughter living in Japan, I'm the closest she has to family. I thought she'd listen to what I had to say. But it was no use.'

'Please tell me this has a happy ending.'

'Well, as a matter of fact, it was talking about Rafa that made me think of her,' Jess replied. 'He told her he was the manager on a construction site with a four-month contract. Then he would come over to be with her. Like Rafa.'

I shook my head miserably as I listened.

'Three months went by and he dominated her every waking moment. She was just willing the time to pass until they could start a life together. He had said he wouldn't move in straightaway, but would rent somewhere close by, so that they could have their space and really get to know each other. That there was no rush, they had their whole lives. Oh boy, did he know the stories to spin. So far, there had been no mention of any money. She felt safe, secure and loved. I kept trying to suggest he wasn't real, but she was in no mind to listen to any of it.'

Jess had been talking with a cup of tea in her hand. Now she put it down to look me square in the eye.

'And then he did it. My nightmare came true. He told her there was a problem with signing the job off, which meant he couldn't pay his workforce. If he couldn't pay his workforce, he couldn't leave Canada. It could mean a delay of six weeks or more. But if she could find a way to help him out, he could repay her as soon as everything was signed off and he could be with her within the week.'

My heart sank. I could guess the rest.

'Don't tell me,' I said. 'She gave him the money.'

Jess nodded.

'Thousands of pounds, without a second thought. Wired to a dodgy, untraceable account, we found out later. Lost forever.'

'And then?'

'And then, he still continued to play the game. For his grand finale. Twisting the knife, I suppose you'd call it. Thanked her, said he had rented a property nearby. Even supplied the address. Said goodnight; he'd see her in three days. And that was it. She never heard from him again.'

'Like Rafa,' I whispered, imagining her pain and shock. 'How did she handle it?'

'She was lost. Baffled. Called me, sobbing, and I got the train straight away. She was a mess, huddled in bed hugging his photo. Convinced he must have broken his phone and would turn up any day. I asked her about the place he said he'd rented. Thank the Lord for that! We looked it up, but it didn't exist. At that, it hit her like a ton of bricks. In a daze, she let me take over and contact the fraud squad, who eventually verified it as a scam.'

'And now?'

'Fine. It was the house that brought her to her senses. When she realised he had made that up, too, her mind went down the line of logic and she saw things differently. She was helping the authorities as much as she could. Shame they couldn't recover any of her savings, but at least she kept her sanity.'

***

It's just so wrong on so many levels. That poor, poor woman. Little did she realise that her profile picture served as a magnet for scammers. A picturesque cottage in the Suffolk countryside? You could smell the pound notes a mile off. A green light for the bad boys.

She had simply created her profile, as anyone would, completely unaware that she was effectively naming herself as a target for scammers.

Sometimes scammers pop up on Facebook. Of course, we all know it's always dodgy to accept friend requests from people you don't know. But we tend to associate romance scams with online dating sites rather than Facebook, yet this has become one of their 'ins'.

Jane, in her seventies, accepted a friend request from a devastatingly handsome Indian. He could have been the lead in a Bollywood movie. He began wooing her with compliments from the off. Incredibly, he spun the relationship out for months before asking for money. He wanted ten thousand dollars to help a child dying of cancer. He supported this with a photo of said child. Poor Jane, not at all affluent, sent the money, even though she had to borrow the last thousand. He was grateful and convinced her to accept money into her account and transfer it out into another foreign account. He never revealed the source of the funds, but as it wasn't her personal money, Jane was happy to comply.

In fact, she was being used as a "money mule." Unbeknown to her, it was other men and women, victims of scams, just like her, who were sending her the money, which she unwittingly transferred across to the scammer's account.

Ironically, it was one of these such victims who reported the scam to the police and Jane's account, as the receiving account, was frozen. The scam came to an end, but the sad fact is that it could have gone on and on.

Jane's case is classic. One of the main reasons that the scams succeed is the lack of awareness on the part of the victims. We jump into relationships expecting the other person to have morals like us, to be who they say they are.

This is an excellent example of where the philosophy "Innocent until proven guilty", can prove to be the downfall of us all.

It's all about raising awareness on a global scale. I, for one, am buying into that. Big time.

CHAPTER 16

Fairy Godmother, Wave your Magic Wand!

So what is being done?

Scams are happening more and more through the internet and email. You're more likely to fall victim to fraud or cyber offences above any other crime.

Well, there is advice out there to avoid being scammed. And there are things you can do to try and get your money back, etc. But to my mind, this is treating it after the event, rather than addressing the root problem; closing the gate after the horse has bolted and all that.

There are various agencies set up to deal with scams all over the world. Plus, of course, the police, fraud squad, etc. In Ireland, for example, the Garda National Cyber Crime Bureau (GCCB) is the national Garda unit tasked with the forensic examination of computer media seized during the course of any criminal investigations — not specifically romance scams, but this would fall under their umbrella. The first point of reference however, is the local police. And let's face it, they have enough on their plate.

Singapore seems to be the global leader of scam investigations. The police set up an Anti-Scam Centre last year to identify and disable scam operations. They work with businesses, financial institutions, telecommunication companies and digital platform owners. To date, it has frozen two thousand six hundred bank accounts and recovered thirty-five per cent of the amount scammed.

Key to this is the centre's ability to work with banks to freeze accounts suspected to be involved in scams within a few days. Previously, this could take as long as two weeks.

Last November, they managed to successfully take down a transnational love-scam syndicate based in Malaysia. Three Nigerian and fifteen Malaysian scammers were arrested, involved in at least one hundred and thirty-nine cases of internet love scams reported in Singapore, Malaysia, Hong Kong and Macau, involving losses of about $5.8 million.

It's a start, but a poor one. And coming at the problem from the wrong angle, in my opinion.

To date, there is no global department to address this at source and actually go after the bastards. Nowadays, with advances in technology, they are sophisticated, organised criminals, working internationally and exploiting their victims to the full.

The technology enables them to set up fake websites, steal people's identities and photos from anywhere in the world, using fake email addresses and fake telephone numbers which are redirected abroad. So they can claim to be in Europe but, in fact, are sitting in a cabin in Ghana.

For the long game, they can spend months grooming victims, getting closer, focusing on emotional issues, developing relationships with those who have had recent relationship breakdowns or a death in the family and more recently, the mental-health problems associated with lockdown and isolation; in other words, people who are easier to mould; who are more gullible.

A classic is getting the victim off the dating site as soon as possible. This is useless for them, other than to source the victim, who seems vulnerable or well-heeled. Once on WhatsApp, Hangouts or private email, they can assume control.

They are able to provide what looks like an authentic bank account to receive the money, but this will be a holding account and any money will be transferred out to their overseas account immediately.

I'm no diplomat, but I'm sure if you sat a dozen random people around a table to debate this for an hour, someone would come up with twice as much than is in evidence today.

For instance, there could be a questionnaire for each and every member of a dating site, to be completed before being accepted, where they are made aware of the statistics of fraudsters and a few red flags to look out for. You could implement this with just five questions. No matter who you are, something will lodge in your brain and maybe open your eyes to the possibility, if nothing else.

This seems minimal in the grand scheme of things but in actual fact, it is huge. Had I been aware, I would have steered away from every single one of my scammers and been spared the pain and stress.

The male scammers are often located in West Africa, while the female scammers are mostly from the eastern parts of Europe.

The money you send to scammers is almost always impossible to recover. Coupled with the shock of all that, you have to deal with the acute sense of betrayal, which often leads to depression or some kind of breakdown. You thought this guy loved you, for heaven's sake.

I ask you, is the above not reason enough to take scamming more seriously? Not enough money is being allocated to invest in educating folk before it happens.

There is a gaping hole in the legal system. This is overlooked, on the increase and will implode. It is a basic infringement of human rights. If even I can see it coming, why is no one doing anything?

These classrooms full of young Africans, sitting on the floor with their laptops, sharing your information with all and sundry, need to be investigated and closed down. It needs to become a criminal offence so that they are locked up for it and lose everything, spending the rest of their miserable lives paying back what they stole. This doesn't cover the trauma they willingly foster, the emotional anguish we go through, the resulting anxiety we suffer, but it helps.

Comeuppance.
Good word that.

CHAPTER 17
Pearls of Wisdom

Every single one of us, at some point in our lives, can become a victim of scammers.

Ha! Everyone except me, I can almost hear you thinking as you read. And for your sake, I hope you're right.

Don't forget, they are masters of the long game, of which the essential ingredient for success is getting the timing right. When to strike. Excuse my French, but they resort to clever psychological shit designed to fuck with your brain. Add the element of surprise to the mix and they are already halfway there. They rely on you not expecting it. Of course, if you have a conscience, which covers the majority of modern society, then all the better. They pile on the pressure for you to help out those you love; i.e., them.

There are certain types of people who fit their brief more than others. And it's not rocket science either. The psychological profile of the most gullible victims is neither complex nor in-depth.

Let's see. By and large, she is single/separated; middle-aged/older; well-educated, looking for someone to be the one to love; desperate/responsive to flattery; more vulnerable.

I cannot stress enough that scammers know the name of the game. They've got aces up their sleeve and know all the tricks in the book to convince you they are the real deal.

It is vital, therefore, that you go into battle prepared, rather than defenceless. And your greatest weapon? Why, information of course!

If you are on the lookout for red flags, can recognise the warning signs and the script, you could avoid months of mental anguish and maintain a healthy bank balance into the bargain. Worth a second thought, don't you think?

To this end, I have compiled a directory of pearls of wisdom.

It is said that if you know your enemies and know yourself, you will not be imperiled in a hundred battles; if you do not know your enemies but do know yourself, you will win one and lose one; if you do not know your enemies nor yourself, you will be imperiled in every single battle.

Sun Tzu, 'The Art of War.'

Sun Tzu was a Chinese general, military strategist and philosopher from the sixth century BC. Yes, that's right: Before Christ. And I can find no better pearl of wisdom than his for today's oh-so high-tech, twenty-first century, modern society.

So let's crack on and delve into the secret strategies of these slimy scumbags.

Do you use your real name on your profile?

Rule of thumb: Don't give anything away so publicly. Think of a username and only reveal your real name further down the line, when you feel comfortable. Protect your privacy. No one else will.

Do you receive eloquent morning messages? Are they personal to you?

If you can confidently answer yes and no to the above questions, mark it as a red flag. Scammers have access to a huge bank of scripts and templates. The majority of the text used is usually a script. They can be short, romantic greetings or longer messages, outlining what they are looking for in a relationship. Always general.

It's easy to identify. There will be nothing related to you in there, or anything you have in common. Ask yourself this: could he send this to *any* woman?

If you are texting and he sends like one of these in a nanosecond, that should also trigger the red alarm bell. If you are still wondering, you can always copy and paste the message into Google and see if it already exists elsewhere.

Some criminal gangs have their 'manuals' — I kid you not! The Bible or the Koran in any other language.

Yes indeed, the source of many of their templates and scripts originate from the following books:

The Game, by Neil Strauss; For You, My Soulmate, by Douglas Pagels.

Are they abroad on contract work, with dodgy internet connection?

A general in the US military, an engineer on a ship, an IT guy offshore on an oil rig, a doctor working in Iran for the UN. All classic occupations from which to base their web of lies and deceit.

Are they widowed with a child?

Classic sympathy card. Some may have romantic photos of their ex and child to show how devastated they were when this precious family unit was so cruelly destroyed.

The wife died during childbirth, but they don't provide much detail and brush over this.

Are they devout Christians?

They often wax lyrical in their faith in the Good Lord, how they have got over their tragedy with prayer and contemplation.

Do they show more than a casual interest in your online dating experience?

These days, they are employing more sophisticated tricks to throw you off the scent. They will ask you if you have had any bad experiences so far. If you say yes, they will want to know how you handled it. Then they will say they want a video call to make sure YOU are real!

This has actually happened to me. The guy, claiming to be an American on a ship, played a video of someone in a sort of control room. I could hear his voice but the mouth was not quite in sync with his words and it lasted less than a minute. He then said it was a bad connection, that he could lose his job if found to be making video calls from there, but that he had to be sure I was for real!

In my case, alarm bells were ringing right round the room and I blocked him. But I am aware that others may have refined the technology to produce some sort of video on a link that plays out for a couple of minutes of your dream guy and, say, his daughter, smiling and laughing at the camera, waving and asking how you are.

Catch them out. Ask a question. No, in fact bombard them with questions. They won't be able to answer and later, won't have an excuse if you asked more than one.

Do they ask you to move away from the dating website on the first day?

Often, they will send a scripted standard message, on the lines of: 'I was really attracted by your profile picture and would love to know more about you. Working abroad, it is difficult to log onto the dating site and emails are far more convenient. If it is no bother to you, send me an email and we can really get to know each other well. Looking forward so much to your reply.'

Or they will ask you to chat on Hangouts. This makes it easier for money transfers further down the line. And of course, you can exchange photos.

Do they call you 'dear?'

A common trait is for them to ditch your real name and call you 'dear', or 'babe'. Far less work for them with their 'dear' and 'babe' scripts. It didn't work for me. Unwittingly, I asked Rafa not to call me either, but instead use my name. Now I realise he had to mess with the script just for me. Shame I didn't catch onto that at the time.

Do they start nurturing the idea of strong feelings in the first few days, showering you with compliments, so that after a week they feel that they are 'falling in love' with you?

This is to rush the emotional stage through, past first base. They even have a damned name for it. Grooming. We are being groomed to accept that it is possible for someone to fall in love so quickly that love at first sight actually does exist.

Although it's not at first sight, because they never agree to video calls. Their voice, photos and flattery, combined with persistence and patience, seem to get them exactly what they want.

Rule of thumb: don't let your feelings run away with you before you have met this person face to face. Before that, anything you have between you is virtual. Nothing else. Keep that at the forefront of your mind, no matter how damned handsome, rich or perfect-for-you he may seem. Maintain your self-respect. Wish I had!

Do they want to retire or relocate to where you are?

This is a biggie. Of course, you might have relatives, friends, a life where you are. How perfect for your Prince to come riding right into your world on his white charger. What could be better?

Do they talk about meeting up after the grooming stage; say, a couple of weeks down the line?

Don't worry, something will come up. A hitch, a setback, a small financial problem. They feign panic and then, lapping up your well-intentioned sympathy and moral support, solve the problem.

Or they could ask for a pay card to cover their internet bill. Anything not too threatening, a birthday gift or a phone.

This has a name, too. Testing the waters. Judging your reaction. If you are enthusiastic in your support, they can move up to the next level. Rearrange the meet. Then stage the disaster. A death, an accident, a child needing urgent surgery. At this point, they bring up the subject of money. They always say it is for a short period of time until they can resolve the problem.

Often, they will give you access to their bank account statement online and the balance is usually in the millions. You feel fine then, just wiring a few hundred dollars or a thousand. It's just to help him out. You'll get it back soon enough.

Rule of thumb: do not send money to anyone you meet online and have not met face to face. Overseas payments via wire transfer, Western Union or Moneygram are generally not possible to trace. Bank accounts are no assurance that they are who they say they are. They forge their identities or use another victim's account, who is inadvertently laundering money.

Do they request intimate photos?

If you comply, you are stepping on shaky ground. This gives them ammunition to shoot you down in flames by means of blackmail. Even headshots can be doctored these days.

Rule of thumb: think twice.

Are they having trouble moving their money?

They want to transfer thousands of dollars out of the country. Or they have gold. They offer you a share and ask if you will receive it for them. Mid-transit, you are hit with shipping taxes of thousands. The money never arrives and you have been scammed.

Once you realise you are being scammed, what can you do?

- Block the scammer
- Keep copies of all correspondence and photos
- Remove your Hangouts account; eliminate the conversation and delete all photos
- Report the situation immediately to the police or fraud squad

- Report it to your bank
- Report it to the dating website
- If you have photos of him, do a Google image search at images.google.com to check if they correspond to your guy, or have been stolen, or have been used in romance scams before.

Reach out and join the Facebook scammer sites. Someone may be able to help you identify him:
- Victims of Scamming
- Let's Stop Scammers
- Scammer Scammer Scammer Action Hunter

There is a Facebook dating site I had a look at, which is ninety-nine per cent scammers, called *Fbook Singles Dating App.* Have a good look through the profiles. Hundreds of girls, all with the same sentence — 'Single, looking for a serious relationship' — with their boobs and booty hanging out. Adonis, fit guys, often with a puppy or a cute child and a standard name like John or Richard. Not only that, it's crammed with comments of people complaining about the number of fake profiles. And Facebook does sweet F.A. Hey, ho!

Yeah, right!

- Do a Reverse Image search. A good site for this is tineye.com. By sharing a specific photo, it will then go on to find others like it.

- Tell your family and friends. After the initial shock, the last thing you will feel like doing is admitting what has happened. You are feeling betrayed, blackmailed and stupid at the same time. They call this a Double Whammy, but I would go one further and say it's a Triple.

You've been robbed of your savings, lost your Prince Charming and stripped of your dignity. That's a hefty three in my book.

So it takes guts to stand up and be counted and confide in those close to you. But keeping mum just plays into their greedy little hands. They want you to be secretive. The fewer people who know, the wider the gulf between what is going on and the awareness of it.

Online romance scamming is still largely unrecognised. Examining and developing a definitive psychological profile of both victims and scammers will help identify those at risk. The information should be out there, in every health centre, dentist's surgery, solicitor's office. In our faces and ultimately in theirs. Something has to change. And soon.

We don't just need to raise awareness for us, as potential victims. We want to let them know we are on to them.

And then?

Then we watch them squirm.

***

Looking back at the first pearl, that of Sun Tzu, we are now in possession of armour in the form of knowledge. Knowledge is power, we know. But, as he so rightly points out, if you don't know yourself you could blindly rush in and still be duped. So the best recipe and the best suit of armour is to come clean and be honest with yourself.

It's hard to admit if you're desperate. It sounds so, well, desperate. It's actually just another word to describe 'normal'. I mean, what would you say if asked to define 'normal?' If you have had ups and downs in your emotional life, if the kids have flown the nest, if you are divorced, widowed, single and l for that certain someone, then that longing can evolve into desperation of ever finding Mr Right, with the knock-on effect of vulnerability.

In other words, normal. This is a totally natural progression of behaviour if you are living alone for whatever reason and would prefer to have a lover and life companion.

So let's try, really hard, to break the mould here, to take Sun Tzu's simply stated advice and know both ourselves and our enemy. It's in our hands. Let's put the word out to them all:

'NO TAKERS.'

What's the worst that can happen? Baby, take it from me, you don't want to go there.

CHAPTER 18
Rapunzel

After Rafa, I hung onto José's morning greetings like a crutch. José was the guy I could rely on, who was exactly what it said on the tin, who wouldn't let me down. He fulfilled this role impeccably. Constant, real, genuine. One day, post-Covid, he would motor down and spend a week or so with me and then move on to other distant shores. I couldn't imagine anything better. My anchor, or coping mechanism, to help me come out the other side and be positive.

Barefoot, enjoying the waves sneaking up to catch me as I walked along the water's edge, the future suddenly didn't seem so bleak after all. How could it be, surrounded by such spectacular scenery? My phone bleeped. A WhatsApp message. I'd look at it later, I decided.

The day ran away with me, filled with routine housework and cooking. I had dinner, a couple of glasses of wine and fell into bed. The following morning, there was no familiar beep, indicating my morning message from José. When I picked up my mobile, I noticed an unread message from him the day before.

Smiling, I clicked to open it. I wish I hadn't.

Jacky, I have something to tell you. A couple of weeks ago I met a girl, here in Asturias. We are getting on so well, and today I decided I wanted to give it a go and see where this will take us. So, although we have been in touch every day for almost a year now, and get on well too, I think it only fair that we put a little distance between us in terms of messaging and calls. I need to be upfront with her from the beginning. I am so sorry. You are incredible, funny, unique. But she is the here and now and we are merely some time maybe in the future. With lots of love, José.

You know that sickly feeling in the pit of your stomach? That pretty much nailed it for the whole weekend.

Meanwhile, the second wave of coronavirus peaked on the 8th of November. Local governments maintained the restrictions, concerned about the upcoming Christmas festive period — in Spain for a good deal longer, as presents are traditionally brought, not by Santa Claus in December, but by the Three Kings on January 6th. However, they relaxed border restrictions from the 23rd of December until January for families to be together.

I took advantage of the freedom and drove north to Cataluña to spend Christmas in the company of friends. Although there was a lot of police presence, I wasn't stopped. The journey went smoothly, culminating in a wonderful welcome from good friends. We had a lot of fun, plus long dog walks in the countryside. I went onto Tinder on the second day, and lo and behold, a guy — Miguel Angel — got in touch from the same village. He looked quite distinguished in his photos, a Richard Gere lookalike, with grey hair. I took the bull by the horns and we arranged to meet in the village square at noon. Restrictions meant that coffee bars could only sell takeaway drinks. It was nippy out, but at least not pouring with rain, or windy.

He was on time. We went for the takeaway coffee. Scarf, gloves, a bench in the square and two hot drinks. It was a lovely first date. We exchanged phone numbers and agreed to stay in touch.

The following day, he sent messages and photos of his home and dog, and later he video-called me. He couldn't speak a word of English, but it didn't seem to matter. We laughed a lot and there was certainly something there, lingering between us. The next day, he invited me out for lunch in the town of Tortosa. I cleared it with my friends, who were delighted for me, and agreed to meet. Restaurants were only permitted to open from one thirty p.m. until three thirty p.m. And you had to make a reservation.

We met by the river an hour before opening time and walked up through the streets, around the market, window shopping, sightseeing. At one thirty p.m., on the dot, the restaurant opened its doors to welcome a full house. I was surprised that so many people had ventured out during the pandemic.

The decor was stunning, based on wood, nature, the outdoors. The service was also good. Shame the menu let them down. Famous for the fish, they told us apologetically that they had run out the previous day. What was available was, frankly, sub-standard and tasteless. It irked me, because I hadn't been to a restaurant in ages. But it didn't in any way detract from the company. We had a fabulous afternoon. Miguel Angel walked me back to my car and asked if he could kiss me. Hell yes!

Two days later, rejuvenated by social contact with valued friends, I drove all the way back home to Almería.

For a couple of weeks, Miguel Angel and I kept in touch, but neither of us was stupid. We chatted, aware of the tacit acknowledgment of the as-yet-unspoken reality. That the relationship was a non-starter, dead in the water.

I was the first to broach the subject, and when I did, he didn't beat around the bush. It was almost a relief. For both of us. Out in the open at last. The distance was a problem. I didn't envisage my future away from the coast. It had taken me so long to realise just what gave me inner peace, and I wasn't prepared to give it up and ride off into the sunset with my PP. Too long in the tooth now for that. He was prepared to come down south with his dog and rent for a month, but that would be when border restrictions were lifted, which could be as far away as June. We agreed to knock it on the head. Just like that.

We are all capable of going down the "What if. . ?" road. Thing is, what's the point?

***

Hardly out of the second wave, no more than a few weeks later, the third wave was advancing. A new variant emerged from the UK, followed by another from South Africa. Christmas and New Year had proved to be a huge mistake. As a result, new local lockdowns, rules and restrictions appeared day after day, in place, we were informed, until May 9th. On the upside, vaccines were approved and a programme set up to administer them in three phases, planned from January through to September. This had to be good news, in terms of fewer cases, and also economically.

Stuck at home, locked down, I felt more like Rapunzel locked in a tower than Cinderella dreaming of her Prince. The possibility of meeting Tinder guys any time soon had been whipped away. The knock-on effect was unexpected. Up to this point, I had managed to juggle my Tinder matches successfully, without a great deal of effort. But now, it was a different story entirely. With no meets on the horizon and new matches dribbling in, I was snowed under with men. By that, I mean around twenty-five or so. Trouble was, there wasn't anything I could put my finger on to stop chatting to any of them. They were uniformly polite, interested and under 'normal' circumstances, potential date material. Plus, they all were eager to come and see me as soon as they were able.

A mixture of British and Spanish, the chats evolved into the occasional call, then video-call. Wary, after my previous 'close shaves', I wasn't prepared to let any feelings loose on anyone before a face-to-face meet. They, however, started to let their feelings run away with them, telling me they were falling for me, sending kisses, flower icons, mushy compliments.

Not once did I respond in kind. But this only served to make them try harder. Men love the thrill of the chase, I suppose. Only this time I wasn't playing. I had my feelings firmly under control and not one of them had come close to getting under my skin. Yet.

Until Apolo.

Unfortunate-looking is how I would describe him, judging from his profile pic. Large features, as in high forehead, dark eyes framed by bushy eyebrows, wide nose, full mouth and protruding chin.

He messaged me first and, like many others before him, we exchanged numbers so we could use WhatsApp. The first week we just messaged, but then he called me. His voice was unusually soft, and he spoke slowly and calmly. He was from Brazil but had lived in Spain for years. He said he had lost his job during Covid and had just accepted a job working for Repsol as an IT engineer on an oil rig. He would be flying out to the rig, sixty-seven kilometres off the coast of Tarragona, by helicopter in three days and that the contract was for forty-two days.

Hmm. Two red flags. Oil rig. IT engineer on contract. I wonder? I thought.

He sent me a video of him, explaining how he landed the job and how excited he was. He loved playing guitar and meditating, and the simple things in life. He was interesting. Maybe a tad more than the others. He always told me when he would call and I looked forward to hearing from him.

I'll let it ride. For now, I decided.

Monday dawned: his first day. He sent me a video of him in the helicopter and another landing on the rig. Later, he messaged to say he had been allocated an hour for calls each night in the comms room, at nine p.m.

Rather than flattering me, or being romantic, we spent the time chatting generally, about our day, music, philosophy. He mentioned he wanted to hire a motorhome for a couple of months after the contract and travel around Spain. Maybe I could join him for some of that? I said we would have to wait and see.

Two weeks down the line and I was speaking to Apolo far more than anyone else. He called on the dot each and every night. Then, one night, he informed me he had a house in Brazil he was trying to sell and needed the hour for that.

'No problem. We'll talk the next day.'

He was 'busy' for three days. On the fourth day, he called, full of apologies, saying he had finished all his business now and his time was ours. I thought nothing of it.

When he called the following evening, instead of his usual upbeat tone, he was quiet, withdrawn, upset about something. Rather than drawing it out, I tried to change the subject and lift him out of it, figuring he would tell me if he wanted me to know.

He seemed to resent this.

'I am really upset. Don't you care?'

Oh dear, can't do right for doing wrong.

'Well, I figured if you wanted to share what's bothering you, you would tell me,' I replied.

He started taking deep breaths and blowing out after each one. 'I'm so nervous. Okay, I'll just say it. I'm having trouble with the house sale and I need to have some repairs done before they will sign. Could I borrow two thousand five hundred euros to cover the cost? It would just be for ten days.'

Well, well, well. We had come full circle. The red flags had been exactly that, but I had chosen to overlook them, giving him the benefit of the doubt.

I almost smiled as I shot back, 'Do you think I am so gullible as to fall for this? Really, Apolo? Do you?'

He sounded wounded. 'What do you mean?'

I couldn't help it. I scoffed and almost laughed. 'Let's just put it this way. For your next victim, don't play the nervous card so strongly. You're not very good

173

at it. Incredibly transparent, in fact. Don't reply. I am not remotely interested in anything you have to say. And know this. I WILL report you.'

I put the phone down, shaking from the confrontation. It rang, almost immediately. Apolo. What the—?

Curiosity made me answer.

'What?'

'Jacky,' he said, his voice pleading. 'I just want to say one last thing.'

I waited.

His tone changed to a snarl. In place of the usual, soft, seductive almost whisper, he now shouted, in the worst Spanish, using *palabrotas*, or *tacos* (swear words).

'*¡Hijo de puta! ¡Que te follen! ¡Que te dan por culo! ¡me cago en el coño podrido de tu puta madre! ¡Vete a la mierda!*

Son of a bitch, get f*****d! And up the arse! I shit on your whore mother's rotten c**t! Fuck off!

I gasped as he slammed down the phone.

Wow. Scary. So much so, I burst into tears. I'm silly like that. But somehow, I feel better afterwards.

The next morning, out of curiosity, I looked to see if there were any messages from him. Not only had he removed his name and profile picture, but eliminated our entire conversation log.

If this had been a psychological ploy, he had chosen the wrong girl. After only a few weeks, I wasn't so emotionally dependent on him to be upset he couldn't call. I had other things to do. And to imagine he could reel me in, gain my trust and ask for money, just like that, was— well, ridiculous.

But maybe that was down to my previous experience. Maybe this did, in fact, work with other unsuspecting, less suspicious girls.

I had got away with it. Easily, I realised.

My God, they are everywhere.

I was tired. Tired of the chats without the prospect of a meet any time soon.

I think I'll go back to being Rapunzel. It's not such a bad situation to be in, after all. At least until lockdown ends.

CHAPTER 19
Timon and Pumbaa: Hakuna Matata

Looking back, I now see a gaping hole in my assessment of Tinder matches. You remember — Frogs, Fraudsters, Perverts and Princes. There's a missing link. It's a vital component of the whole package, to boot, never mind slipping easily into the list and significantly enhancing the alliteration.

Throughout Covid, quarantine and numerous lockdowns, I have chatted to so many men, none of whom I could categorise as Frogs, Fraudsters, Perverts or Princes. Of course, my judgement here is subjective, but every one of you out there will find the same, according to your own criteria. And it turns out there's another group out there.

The strange thing is, I never actually realised until months of Tindering. And the reason is simple. No spark.

Nestling cosily in the middle of my list, I have now added a new category: that of 'Friends'.

It takes a while to recognise that, while there may not be a mutual sexual/romantic attraction, you may have been chatting for a few weeks, even months, and have a fair bit in common. On the first date I often had a great time and enjoyed the company but no more than that. Subtly, without realising, a different kind of relationship subconsciously arises. For me, I would say something like, 'Although we seem to get on, I'm not feeling it,' or 'You're a really nice guy, but not my guy.'

And for many, they stopped chatting immediately, were offended, upset, or just accepting. Then, on a few occasions, up to six months later, they would resurface, chatting, and wham! A friendship began to flourish.

Personally, I prefer friends I can physically meet, once we are free to cross borders. So I went with the friendships in the south of Spain, which could be developed post-Covid. But there are lots of you who love having penfriends or video mates, even more so since the pandemic. Most of us can handle some form of video calling and who knows, could get together as friends someday.

Neil and I had our first date a few months back. He drove down to meet me on the beachfront, where we had a beer together. Conversation flowed and the beer evolved into an impressive seafood lunch platter.

An English guy, of all the places he could have been from, he was from the same town as me. I have lived outside the UK on and off for twenty-five years, in Europe and Africa, and never once come across anyone from my little town. Yet there he was in all his glory, sitting across the table sharing lunch.

That fact alone made for quite a few trips down memory lane, secondary schools, local bars, peer groups. He had seemed a little uptight at first, but soon let his guard down and everything just spilled out.

The sun, reflecting on the water, was spectacular. The food was different, freshly caught and mouth-watering. The ambiance was inviting. Yet he didn't stop for breath and these things, for me the essence of the occasion, were overlooked. I said very little and listened. Truth be told, I was feeling a little bombarded, but it wasn't the end of the world. After lunch, he walked me back and drove home. I declined a hug: not Covid-friendly.

Later, I tried to let him down. He said he was blown away, that he knew he had talked too much, but he really believed we could get over this and maybe have something. Would I give him a second chance?

It was true. He certainly wasn't a Frog. Although I had thirteen sub-categories, he didn't fit into a single one. Yet he wasn't my Prince. Or was he?

'Maybe I have been a little hasty,' I thought.

I invited him for lunch the following week. It went well. When he left, I gave him a hug. Over the next couple of weeks, he wrote a song for me and a poem. I was flattered and delighted at the same time. They were so full of passion, love, devotion; the sort of thing romantic girls dream of receiving, from their Prince. It sort of spelled it out to me, that he wasn't my Prince. I didn't get butterflies in my tummy when he called. I didn't fall asleep thinking about him. As much as he fitted the bill on paper, it wasn't happening for me.

So I came clean. Right out with it. He was brilliant. Disappointed, but happy to accept a 'let's-be- friends' deal. And he has proved to be an excellent friend ever since. Dependable, constant, a message or call daily. He has moved on romantically and has met a lovely girl. Doesn't stop us chatting though.

Then there was Pick-up Pedro, so-called due to his wonderful repertoire of pick-up lines. He was a scream, but when he called, his Spanish accent was really difficult to grasp. I only got two or three words.

Houston, we have a problem.

From the off, still on the Tinder site, he had me in stitches with his messages. I was on the verge of suggesting we progress to WhatsApp, when he got in first.

- I think there's something wrong with my phone. Your number's not in it.

Hilarious. He had caught my attention for sure. One morning, he sent this:

- You must be tired from running through my mind all night.'

When I sent him photos, he shot right back with:
- "Aside from being sexy, what do you do for a living?"

After the disastrous phone call, we tried a video call. The make-or-break, as I saw it. Too bad it was the break. Pick-up Pedro could certainly talk the talk, no doubt about that, but boyfriend material he just wasn't. He lived with his seven dogs and as far as I could see, they had the run of the place. There was certainly no room for a woman in his life.

After the call, I was wondering how to tell him. To date, all I had done was laugh, giving out all the wrong signals.

A few hours later, his message came through.

-   If I could rearrange the alphabet, I'd put "U" and "I" together.

For the first time, it didn't raise a smile. I knew I couldn't put it off any longer. I sent a voicemail, saying I didn't feel the same, but thought he was good company, a great laugh and how about we stay in touch as friends?

And do you know what? He agreed. We are still in touch, happy with our set boundaries. Not a Frog, Fraud, Pervert or Prince, but a Friend.

I met Karl soon after moving down here. We arranged to meet for a beer at the beach bar at five thirty p.m. forgetting all about the six-p.m. curfew. We had hardly placed the order when they were packing up the tables around us.

I shrugged. 'Would you like to come to mine for one? You can hardly call this a date.'

I opened a bottle of red. We got on okay, if a little stilted, as he was forever mixing his languages. He was German, anxious to practise his English with me and his Spanish in general. Plus, he was hard of hearing. However, he was very laid-back, polite and friendly. I let him stay over to avoid driving. He left the next morning and for a while, that was it. We didn't message one another. A few weeks later, he got in touch. He was working in the next village, San José, he said. Would I like to come over to a bar in the square for a beer?

I had never been to San José, so I agreed. We met, had a beer and I left. For me, he was a really nice guy I didn't fancy. Again, not a Frog. A potential Friend. We met up once more for drinks one evening. Had a good time, but as friends. The relationship, strangely, seemed to be evolving on its own, without any help. This is the difference between meeting face to face and endless messaging. Things get sorted.

***

It's a cliché, but I truly believe that things happen for a reason. On the morning of 13th January, 2021, I walked eight kilometres, had a coffee at Antonio's bar by the beach and went home to prepare lunch. From out of nowhere, this blinding pain hit me in the top of my stomach, just under my ribs. It made me cry out. It was difficult to breathe. I didn't know whether to sit or stand. Nothing seemed to ease it. Then suddenly my whole body was heaving, retching, with nothing to come out. Then I was sweating madly, then cold. Teeth chattering, body shaking with cold. More retching. I sat upright, sipping water, blowing breaths out, trying to push through the pain.

Long story short, I got myself up to bed, propped up against pillows, snug under the duvet and stayed like that all night until ten a.m. Everything was going through my mind, and I thought it must be trapped wind. However, after twenty long, long hours, I suddenly had a thought.

'Oh my God, what if I'm having a heart attack? What if I'm dying?'

Neil texted me just as the thought struck me. I sent a panic message. Naturally, he picked up the phone and called me. Rasping from the effort of talking, I told him what was going on.

'Look, I can't get to you. It's just short of a two-hour drive and a fine if I get stopped. I'll call an ambulance now. What about that German guy? He lives in your region, doesn't he?' He hung up.

He was right. I called Karl.

'Karl, I'm sick. An ambulance is coming.'

He didn't even ask. 'I am coming' was his immediate reply.

Twenty minutes later, there was a pounding on my front door. The ambulance crew. There was no way I could get out of bed, let alone downstairs, so they broke in through the patio doors at the back. Karl arrived five minutes later, as they were carrying me downstairs in a chair and into the ambulance.

'What do you need?' Karl called out.

'Orange purse with health card, door key, phone, yellow bag. Thank you,' I croaked back, trying not to scream out when they moved me.

They rushed me to hospital where I underwent emergency surgery for a perforated stomach ulcer. All those hours it had ruptured my colon and been infecting the rest of my body. My kidneys were failing, I developed peritonitis and was in ICU for five days. Karl followed the ambulance, but was refused entry, so he left my things with a nurse. With over one hundred staples forming a long scar down my stomach, I was discharged far too early, to make way for Covid patients. Unable to walk, Karl came to the rescue, taking me home and getting a little shopping in for me. But then he was off and left.

In desperation, I googled the number of Antonio's bar. That wonderful man dropped everything and rushed over to help. He took me to the Health Centre, to have my wound dressed. I was so grateful. I didn't know a soul other than him.

The staff at the Health Centre in the village deserve the Nobel Prize. The nurse took one look at me and said she would come to my home to change my dressing. Every weekday. That was Friday. On Sunday, the staples began leaking blood. I cleaned the wound as best I could. On Monday, the nurse duly came round, removed the dressing and gasped. A thick, dark brown liquid was oozing out. She took a photo, sent it to the doctor, who picked up the phone and ordered an ambulance!

A bacterial infection, that's what! The surgeon removed some staples at the top of the wound and tried to flush out as much as she could with syringes of saline. Then she packed it with gauze soaked in iodine and sent me home.

Sitting alone working out the best way to get to the kettle, the doorbell rang. An English couple, Maggie and Tony, who lived in the village, had heard of my plight from Antonio and decided to find me and see if I needed any help. Angels sent from Heaven, both of them. Maggie went round tidying up, while Tony did the shopping. We had a cuppa and exchanged numbers and they proved more than once to be my lifeline over the following weeks.

That was six weeks ago. On the road to recovery, I am now much more independent and can do most things other than heavy lifting, stomach exercises and driving. For the first three weeks of being ill, I hadn't responded to messages from my twenty-five or so guys, only having the energy for family and close friends. When I finally looked, only six had hung in there.

A bit extreme, but I suppose that's one way of sifting out the good'uns.

What happened to me that day, January 13th, could have been my last, but for my Tinder Friends, who came through for me. I would have sat it out in agony until it was too late. But the second I reached out to him, Neil called an ambulance. Later, sent home far too early, I would never have managed that first day without the kindness of Karl.

So the moral of the story is: when you know he's neither your Prince nor a Frog, don't cut him off and block him forever. Plop him in the Friend category. He may just come through for you one day.

The quote about friends that made an impression on me was by A.A. Milne:

"If ever there is tomorrow when we're not together… there is something you must always remember. You are braver than you believe, stronger than you seem, and smarter than you think. But the most important thing is, even if we're apart… I'll always be with you."

— Winnie the Pooh

CHAPTER 20
Hidden in Plain Sight

It's a funny thing, but so many times we fail to notice something right under our noses, simply because we are neither looking for, nor expecting it. And then when it is revealed to us, we wonder how on earth we never clocked it before. A bit like optical illusions.

It was a beautiful afternoon, August 2020. I was busy packing up my house and thoroughly bored of being inside. A cold beer would hit the spot, I thought.

I messaged Daisy in the village and agreed to meet her and hubby Luke in the village bar. It was only a few minutes' walk. I arrived first. Another English couple, Orla and Bill, were sitting outside.

'Hiya Jacky! Come and join us.'

'Don't mind if I do.'

'So are you all set?' asked Orla, with a smile.

I shrugged. 'Just about. Thank God you agreed to come down and help, Bill. I need your muscle to shift all the furniture.'

'Don't worry, we'll have you sorted in no time.' Bill stood up to go to the bar. 'What are you drinking?'

I turned to see Daisy and Luke walking down the hill. It was only six o'clock.

'Oh, the hell with it. I'll have a glass of red thanks.'

An hour later, conversation drifted to online dating and a few of my recent exploits. Pre-Pervert week, my experience to date had been mostly of the Frog category. Lots of laughs later, Daisy suddenly piped up.

'Well, Yours Truly has no complaints.'

I looked up. 'You mean—?'

She nodded. 'I sure do. May I present Luke, my POF Prince.'

OMG. I was looking at a real-life Prince Charming. We had been friends for over a year now and I had never realised.

'You're not the only one.' Orla was giggling and gazing into Bill's eyes.

'No! You two, as well? Dark horses, the lot of you. My round, I believe.'

***

Intrigued by the fact that right on my doorstep, in this area of Spain, nestling in the middle of olive groves in the Andalucian hills, two of the couples I had grown close to had met online and were crazy about each other. I mean it wasn't as if we lived in a highly populated, bustling city. The chances were at best, slim. And yet, here they were, living, breathing examples of the 'Happy Ever After' fairy tale.

I wanted to find out more. We were the same kind of people. We had clicked straight away. So what on earth was I doing wrong? There must be a secret ingredient, or something elusive that was certainly eluding me. Maybe they could shed light on it for me.

'Come on then, Orla. Dish the dirt.' We were alone, spending a girly afternoon together.

She looked at me and chuckled. 'Not a lot of dirt to dish if I'm honest. I was lucky to find my Mr Right quite early on.'

'So what's your secret? I mean, I don't have a long list of must-haves. Just a like-minded, ambitious guy who I fancy. It's been months and frankly, more like a needle in a haystack than anything else. It's enough to throw in the towel.'

Orla shook her head. 'Just keep at it. And be careful. Maybe you have more things on your tick list than you realise. I mean, be honest, how real is it? Do you have this starry-eyed image of a smart, romantic, financially independent guy?'

'Well, of course,' I shot back. 'Those things are a given. I'm too long in the tooth and have been stung too many times to launch into a relationship with anyone without those qualities. Plus a few more to boot! What was on your checklist?'

'Oh, just a kind, honest guy who was prepared to get to know the real me,' came the gentle reply.

'So how did you get into online dating? Were you coerced into it by your daughters, like me?'

'Ha ha, not exactly. It was my friend, Sita, a work colleague. But it took some time to convince me, I have to say.'

'How so?'

'Well, she knew I was single, didn't go out much and not of a mind to know how to go about meeting anyone. So she suggested the app, Plenty of Fish. I remember just scoffing and laughing in her face, telling her that those online dating sites were for sad, desperate women and she could leave me out of it, thank you very much. But this didn't deter her. She kept reminding me about the odds of her ever finding love that way, and what had happened to her; that most people I knew of my age were married. How else did I expect to meet anyone? I couldn't deny it, and in the end, I caved in.'

'So what did happen to her?'

'Sita is Moroccan and Moslem. She started online-dating, prepared to wait a long time to find someone. She was choosy, with a long line of boxes to be ticked. She was right — it did take a while, but she persisted and is now extremely happy, in love and engaged to her Prince.'

'Good for her. So why didn't you have much of a social life?'

'Well, for starters, it wasn't as if I had my own place. I was living with my daughter and son-in-law, and feeling like a spare part. My paltry social life revolved around their friends, a whole generation younger. It felt like they were Granny-sitting and I was waiting for God in the corner. Through nobody's fault, purely down to circumstances, I had no life of my own and no clue as to how to go about getting one.'

She smiled ruefully. 'Until, that is, when Sita bullied me into doing something about it So, having given in, she helped me set up a decent profile, using a great photo of me at a wedding, all dolled up. I didn't go for any of the payment options. Just wanted to test the waters and use the free part of the site.'

'So how did it go?'

'Well, I had a few teething problems,' she admitted. 'Lots of messages from abroad popped up, from the US military, who were really complimentary from the off and who I began responding to. Sita was supervising me though and warned me against these guys. I had no idea and was happy to take her advice and leave them all alone. So then I focused on local guys who I could video call using WhatsApp. I spent three to four months chatting to this one particular guy, trying to get the hang of it, still not ready to go to the next level, as in an actual face-to-face meet, which eventually fizzled out. I mean, let's face it, if I wasn't going to meet them, then where could the relationship go? Time to give myself a pep talk.

'Right, the next guy who pops up, I'll suggest a meet,' she went on. 'Public place, not local. A bar. And I did. He turned up, thank God, looking posh in his cravat, but it was soon crystal clear that there was no connection there. Plus, his story about being a businessman who dealt in jewellery didn't ring true. After that date, he suggested another, but I didn't reply. However, the thing I took away from the experience was that meeting is the way forward. No more chatting for weeks on end, I told myself. I changed the goalposts.'

'Good for you!'

'I know. After two marriages, I wasn't particularly looking for 'The One', as in a full-on, long-term relationship, but rather to expand my social circle and have a bit of fun. That week, I met a guy who seemed to fit the bill and we went out two or three times. He said he wanted what I had thought I did. But whereas for him that translated as meeting girls, having fun and sex, it fell somewhat short of my personal interpretation of 'expanding my social circle and having fun'. How many other girls would I be sharing him with? I made a hasty retreat.'

I laughed out loud. 'Another goalpost change?'

Orla nodded. 'You betcha. Now, I decided to look for someone who would commit just to me. The next guy was— well, okay, sweet, but a bit of a Mummy's boy. A delivery man. After his divorce, he moved in with Mum.'

I nodded. 'Frog number three.'

'What?'

'Never mind. I suppose that didn't work out either?'

'No. I began to suspect he wasn't all he said he was. Always made excuses not to introduce me to his mum,

191

etc. I broke it off. Straight after that, I was subjected to a guy texting smutty stuff. I was really fed up. "If you want that kind of thing, you need to put your hand in your pocket, and baby, I am way too pricey for the likes of you." That's what I wrote. Honestly.

'By this time — so frustrated — I was on the point of coming off the site and giving it all up as a bad job. If the next guy is a plonker, then that's me done. For good. Thankfully, the next guy turned out to be my Bill,' she beamed.

'I forgot everything that had happened before. Bill, new to the site, lived and worked with men and simply wanted some females in his social circle. After only a couple of days chatting, we agreed to meet in the local pub up the road. It was cold and pouring down so, all dolled up in my fur coat, I drove. In the car park, I texted, "Here in a blue Merc." There was a knock on the window and there he was, a huge smile all over his face. I was pleasantly surprised and the evening went from strength to strength. I remember him saying, quite early on, "All fur coat and no knickers." All too soon it was last orders. I didn't want the evening to end so we moved on to a curry house. We held hands, I fancied him like crazy…' She paused, remembering. 'Yes, instant chemistry.' She handed me a drink. 'And the rest is history. Going strong for three years now, living the dream in Spain. What could be better?'

She was absolutely right.

***

Well, it seemed there was no single magic spell to chant; no "sure thing" at the end of the line; no set formula for success in the online dating game. Orla had got it right after only a few hiccups, whereas here I was scaling peaks and avoiding boulders. Would Daisy's story prove any different?

'I love your coffee.'

Daisy had a great coffee machine and used it all the time. We sat out on her stunning terrace, overlooking rows of olive trees in the middle of the Andalucian hills, an ideal place to hear her story.

Single for two years, in her forties, Daisy was in a rut. Her rut consisted of working and going to the gym and very little social life otherwise. There were certainly no men at the gym who she would ever describe as 'marriage material.'

'Online dating was something I just decided to try out. I told myself, "What have you got to lose?"'

She laughed. 'As it turned out I had everything to gain.'

'I was very selective,' she went on. 'I was careful with my questions, and messaged a couple of chats for around three weeks, plus video calls, before finally meeting them. The first guy was a no-no. The second had potential, which led to a second date, but that was it after that. He wasn't the one. And then I met Luke.'

'Wow, you don't mess around.'

Daisy laughed. 'The thing is, we had a lot going for us before we even met. As we both worked for the NHS, we had moved in the same social circles and had a lot in common. Plenty to get on with on a date, at least. At that point he felt like a safe bet.'

'Oh dear, that sounds ominous. What do you mean, "at that point"? Did things change for the worse before they got better?'

'No, no not at all. I just meant that having so much in common clinched it for me. We quickly set up a date in a pub. It lasted only a couple of hours, but that was enough to know it felt right. Just right. When a bouquet of flowers arrived from him the following day, it was YES! We launched into a whirlwind romance. We were in love, crazy for each other.'

'Wowsers! Bye-bye online dating. Thanks for the add. Objective achieved.'

'Absolutely. At first, we spent weekends in a static caravan in the Cotswolds. Luke is an ardent Villa supporter so we used to watch the footie on Saturdays. As I was living with my Mum, I often stayed over at his and then, three months down the line, he asked me to move in. Problem was, he lived in a typical man cave, not really conducive to female presence of any kind. So we looked around for an alternative. As luck would have it, a friend was letting his four-bedroom house in Birmingham. A cracker of a house, perfect for us, with three kids between us and at a decent price. We just snapped it up, without really giving it much thought, as the next natural step. We stayed there for six months, still crazy in love, and decided to buy a cottage in Bidford on Avon, near Stratford. We were both over the moon, working hard and having something to show for it and someone to share it with. Then I was made redundant. The lease for the local pub came up for grabs, which we took on.'

She paused. 'We had been together for two years when he sprung it on me.'

'What?' I was imagining all sorts.

'He sat me down one evening and proposed. I had never been more sure of anything in my life.

"Daisy, Daisy, give me an answer do;
I'm half crazy
All for the love of you.
It won't be a stylish marriage,
I can't afford a carriage.
But you look sweet
Upon the seat
Of a bicycle made for two."

'This was a proposal. One with a difference. The element of surprise. He revealed that he had arranged everything. Guess where? Only Gretna Green!'

She clapped her hands. 'All I had to do was sort my dress. He had sorted the chapel, the ceremony, had rings engraved, the reception, hotel and rooms for eight guests, everything. It was perfect. We were on cloud nine. Returning to reality, we struggled with the pub and with the recession in 2013, the bottom fell out of the market. Long story short, we had to surrender the lease and sell our beautiful home to pay it off. We ended up in a static caravan for eighteen months with Luke working another job. Eventually, we made the move to Spain before Brexit hit. Finding this place has been the jewel in the crown. We have everything to live for, but I know one thing for sure.'

'What's that?'

'True love doesn't depend on being rich or poor or where you live. It's about taking what comes at you together, working hard and appreciating what you have. And I have that and more in Luke.'

Daisy too, like Orla before her, was absolutely right.

A simple truth. Too often overlooked.

This is Daisy
Daisy used online dating sites the right way
Daisy used video chats and met face to face
Daisy found her Prince
Be like Daisy.

There she was, right under my nose. My friend Daisy. Who had used online dating in the safest, most sensible way possible. She had sourced matches in her local area and made sure she spoke to them via video chats before actually meeting them in a public place.

The KISS method. Keep It Simple, Stupid. Scheherazade, from wench to queen. Daisy used the site to her advantage and is reaping the reward with her real-life Prince Charming.

Come full circle.

And there it was. My answer. Staring me full in the face. Hidden in plain sight.

Do a Daisy.

***

Never too late. My journey had been exhausting, it's true. From the off, it was daunting. But with Daisy's help, I was determined to hold out, to keep it simple until I met that guy. You know, the one who would bowl me over, maybe not from the off, but who would fall squarely into the PP category: Potential Prince. I wasn't greedy. I required only the one.

Everything in life boils down to faith, I told myself. My guy is most definitely out there. We will find each other. I must remember to remain dignified, patient and wise. Then I will be Queen.

With this new mindfulness (the ubiquitous word of the moment), I moved this thought forward from subconscious desire to encompass the raw reality it could prove to be. I was going to walk the walk.

That night I did something I haven't dared or remotely wanted to do for many months. I stripped off and stood naked in front of the full-length mirror in my bedroom.

Well, if you are intending on finding your prince, this is what he has to fall in love with, I thought, with a huge sigh. Never mind the scar all the way down my belly. That was the least of my concerns. At least that was temporary. No more hiding.

Sex. It was going to have to be brought to the table, no pun intended. It had been a while. And even then, it's far more daunting getting naked with someone new.

What I was afraid of, I realised, was falling short; of disappointing. Every woman, whatever shape or size, wants to be desired, passionately, unconditionally. Traditionally, you wait for the man to pursue you. At least, that's the way I was planning on playing it, that's for sure. And it's at that point, I have to be mindful and accepting of the simple truth. You have faith in him to get as far as the bedroom... or the table (couldn't resist!). Have faith in YOU, to respond in kind and have the ride of your life. And be happy ever after.

Armed with all of this positive thinking, all done within the five short minutes as I surveyed myself in the mirror, I pulled on my PJs with renewed vigour.

A fresh cuppa and a session on Tinder awaits, methinks.

I secured five matches, no less, that evening, all of whom started up a chat. A Frenchman, two Spanish and two English. All within an hour-and-a-half's drive, complying with the "Daisy approach".

Anthony stood out straight away. Light years away from the others. His messages, rather than one-liners, were friendly, non-threatening, interesting and chatty. We quickly progressed to WhatsApp. The other four remain on the Tinder site, penning a couple of one-liners a day.

It was clear that Anthony was actively exploring the scope of his matches; in this particular instance, lil 'ole me. After a few messages, he asked if he could call. I was strangely excited. I usually balk at video calls, but with my new approach, I had to throw such inhibitions to the wind.

'So be it,' I thought.

He was charming, in a modest way. Engaging, witty, interested, funny. In other words, the call was a success. He lived in the same province and had an appointment in the city two weeks away. When he suggested coming to see me afterwards, I didn't hesitate.

Crikey. A date. A real, live, proper date. With someone who I obviously liked, due to the nerves I was feeling. Well, the good thing was, I had two weeks for my scar to heal up even more. Two weeks to be calm and ready. Perfect.

Until he called the following day. Our chat lasted an hour and a half. Not one to throw endless compliments out there, although I really enjoyed chatting, I wasn't sure if he was feeling it like I seemed to be.

It was the little things that provided the answer. A comment here, a message there. I was slowly grasping it. Romantic in the mushy sense he was not; rather he made himself known subtly. He suddenly came out with how much he was looking forward to meeting and how two weeks seemed like a long way away. How did I feel about a meeting earlier, like in four days' time?

He caught me off guard, so I was surprised to hear my 'Daisy' personality reply, without skipping a beat.

'I can't wait. Would you like to meet in the village square?'

***

The manual according to Daisy states:
- video chat sooner rather than later
- local meet
- if you don't like him, move on
- be prepared to open your heart if he floats your boat

Anthony ticks all of the above boxes. We had such a great day, doing the thing I love most, walking along the water's edge on a warm, sunny day, chatting animatedly, sitting on a couple of fenders looking out to sea, watching the waves. Moving up to the bar for a beer and fish tapas, which we happily shared with the resident moggies. Back to my place and a light lunch, followed by a drive along the coast road. He never once lunged at me, declared undying love or even tried to kiss me. We were simply enjoying each other's company and paving the way for better things to come. When he left, with a long hug, I was relieved.

Relieved that all the impulsive, impatient moves he could have so easily made had not been on the agenda. Relieved that the gate remained wide open for a possible rosy future.

The following morning, I received another cheery, chatty message, but he headed it up by saying how good he felt, that he was thinking of me, that his life was looking sunnier.

Well, in my book, you can't ask better than that. This could be the guy who sees beyond the image in the mirror, the guy I want to have sex with, and lots of it. Yes, with a hole in the upper part of my stomach, and a scar snaking its way from there all the way down, I am feeling sexy. Ready to get back in the game.

Thank you, Daisy, from the bottom of my heart.

Have I found my Prince Charming? Well, let's just say, from where I'm standing, it's looking good so far.

I really hope so.

Trust me, I'm crossing everything I've got, except my legs.

END